BLACK POWER
AND URBAN UNREST

BLACK POWER
AND URBAN UNREST
Creative Possibilities

by Nathan Wright, Jr.

Hawthorn Books, Inc.   Publishers   New York

To
BARBARA
power person in my life

CONTENTS

I

Power and Conscience

The Black Power issue in American life was raised early in the summer of 1966 in a manner which was clearly as frightening as it should have been understandable. Regardless of these circumstances, the power issue and the creative possibilities inherent in the concept of Black Power may provide a key to new approaches to a number of increasingly critical problems related to the nation's urban life. These creative possibilities are the subject of this book. Their examination may be used for the larger good of the whole nation as it clarifies the Negro's newly intensified positive efforts to use his latent strength for America's enrichment.

An Anguished Cry

The call for Black Power, raised early in the summer of 1966, was a desperate and anguished cry of utter frustration on the part of some whose hopes for a better America had led them to participate in the James Meredith march for voter registration in Mississippi. The expression had about it several surface qualities which, understandably, bred alarm.

1

It was perceived as a form of defiance; and such it was. It was an instantaneous breakthrough of a long-nurtured and long-developed recognition that, in some way, some new form of power in the service of justice must come face to face with the clear and unabated abuse of power.

The issue had a built-in color quality. The long-standing, ineffectively challenged, and misused power was exercised by white people. Those receiving the butt end of that power were black. Those who marched through the unreconstructed backroads of Mississippi saw at almost every hand signs of the utter defiance of America's laws. They sensed that those who misused power to keep the Negro from the exercise of his voting and other civil rights were determined that such defiance would continue. It was clear to these doubtless far too idealistic marchers for human rights that Negroes, who were powerless before the continued injustices of the powerful, needed power.

Without conscious forethought or analysis, some of the younger participants in the voter-registration march rallied others with the age-old expression of the Negro's yearning that his condition be marked by more than weakness. Almost instinctively their pathetic anguish gave voice to the cry "Black Power!"

People who heard the cry when it was first raised report feelings of both understanding and apprehension. Clearly the powerless black people of rural Mississippi—and throughout the land —needed power. Yet this was a new cry. It represented a new stance which, under the potentially explosive conditions of parts of the rural South and our northern slums, could herald a threatening imbalance in the power relationships through which progress had been previously charted.

The continuation of the cry quickly made clear that the fears were justified, at least in part. Old mechanisms for the purpose of work for racial progress were being challenged and judged ineffective. Under the banner of Black Power, and in the manifest breakdown of patience, long-trusted and acknowledged

Negro leaders were being bypassed, if not disclaimed. White leaders were being set aside. There was a breach in the tried and time-worn mechanisms for communication.

What did this new mood represent? Would it create a chain reaction of violence in the rural South and make for more unrest in the northern and southern city streets? Who would act as representatives of these unfamiliar forces that were crying "Black Power?" To the national uneasiness from the growing tensions of several previous long, hot summers, the Black Power scare added an even deeper ominous feeling. Black Power had thus come before the nation as the symbol and source of apprehension and defiance.

It was under a gathering cloud of national gloom that the National Committee of Negro Churchmen was called together on July 22, 1966.

Many of the forty-odd churchmen who met at the Bethel African Methodist Episcopal Church in Harlem had not known each other personally, and most had not shared with each other their ideas or uneasiness concerning the issue of Black Power. Yet all of them were learned men who knew and participated in the Negro's common historical experience. The call to the meeting had simply asked each to come in response to the public controversy over Black Power. Some came with prepared statements and suggestions of resolutions. All were deeply concerned with the controversy and were mindful of the national distress raised by the issue of Black Power. Significantly, however, there was an almost totally unexpected unanimity. Every churchman present recognized the need—for the good of the Negro and for the larger good of the whole nation—of the positive implications of the concept of Black Power. They saw that an anguished and alarming cry, reflecting gross malfunctions in the life of the nation, could serve a re-creative role so desperately needed in America today. In their one-day meeting, the assembled churchmen began to examine the possibilities of this role.

Distortions of Truth

A number of churchmen presented positive statements concerning Black Power. The fundamental theme of all of the presentations was that the current controversy over Black Power was a logical consequence of historic distortions of truth in American life. The spirit of some was initially pessimistic. But particularly evident was the feeling expressed by others that the seeming darkness of the present moment could, if used to good advantage, herald a new day of truth and understanding so long needed in the nation's life. This latter spirit soon prevailed, and the corporate energies of the group led to the release of a thoroughly irenic but nonetheless compelling statement under the caption "Black Power," which appeared in a three-quarter-page advertisement in *The New York Times* of Sunday, July 31, 1966. (The text of the statement comprises Appendix A of this book.)

The greatest historic distortion of truth with respect to the black people of America was seen to be in regard to the use of power and conscience. Negroes have been led to assume that their only right of appeal to white Americans as individuals or to America as a whole was through the agency of conscience, the clergymen concluded. On the other hand, it has been assumed that to white people alone belongs the option of enlisting power to secure one's ends.

Considerable discussion of the place of power in the lives of Negroes was summed up in the words: "Powerlessness breeds a race of beggars." The churchmen who were present saw in the equitable extension of power throughout the whole of American life the one and only key to the preservation of the foundations of the nation. The formal statement of the churchmen declared at this point: "The power of white men is corrupted because it meets little meaningful resistance from Negroes to temper it and keep white men from aping God. The conscience of black men is corrupted because, having no power to implement the demands of conscience, the concern for justice is transmuted into a distorted form of love, which, in the absence of justice, becomes chaotic self-surrender."

The issue raised here seems to go to the heart of so many of our failures in efforts for the advancement of black people. For no other group in America has there been the concerted and sustained plea for sympathy and love as there has been for Negroes. Other groups have sought, or have been led to seek, not love but justice. Within the framework of justice, love may bring fulfillment to human relationships. Without justice, love can only be acquiescence. Negroes have been asked and led to submit in their relationships with white Americans. Yet it is only through a balance of strengths that honest interrelationships may be fostered. Conscience may speak to conscience; power alone may address itself effectively to power. This has been true for all ethnic groups in America, save the Negro. "The fundamental distortion facing us in the controversy about 'black power,' " so the churchmen held, "is rooted in a gross imbalance of power and conscience between Negroes and white Americans."

Using as a background the historic distortions of conscience and power in relation to the Negro in America, the churchmen addressed portions of their statement to four groups of people for whom clarification was seen to be of the "most urgent necessity."

Freedom and Opportunity

To the leaders of America, the churchmen spoke of the evident absence of power on the part of Negro Americans to fulfill or to realize *in life* as well as *in law* the opportunities which are the rightful inheritance of all Americans. The concept of Black Power was seen as a reminder "of the need for and the possibility of authentic democracy in America." They saw the difficulties in America's not coming into its own as stemming from the "inequality of power."

The Committee of Negro Churchmen saw the growing urban unrest as the expression of judgment upon a nation for its failure to use its abundant resources for the common good. In a pointed way the problems of our central cities were placed at the feet of the decision-makers in the white middle-class suburban community for their doubtless unconscious misuse of power. The statement reads: "We deplore the overt violence of riots, but we believe it is more important to focus on the real causes of these eruptions. These sources may be abetted inside the ghetto, but their basic causes lie in the silent and covert violence which white middle-class America inflicts on the victims of the inner city. The hidden, smooth and often smiling decisions of American leaders which tie a white noose of suburbia around the necks and which pin the backs of the masses of Negroes against the steaming ghetto walls—without jobs in a booming economy; with dilapidated and segregated educational systems in the full view of unenforced laws against it; in short: the failure of American leaders to use American power to create equal opportunity *in life* as well as *in law*—this is the real problem and not the anguished cry for 'black power.' "

White suburbanites often feel stunned and wounded when the root of problems is seen to lie with them. This is understandable; and yet they cannot claim to be blameless. Later chapters will develop the theme that only when greater use is made of the latent strength within the Negro community will others respond to the Negro in substantially more effective ways. The aggressive confrontation by the Negro churchmen of the leaders of America may be understood as simply a beginning of the display and use of latent power within the Negro community. Yet whether or not Negroes demand the respectful attention and effective participation at all levels in American life which they are due, the consequences for all of America unless they get them remain the same. The denial of free access to opportunity will lead America closer to self-destruction. We cannot create two Americas—one of want and the irresponsibility born of desperation and another of callous affluence—and still build and sustain one nation, under God, indivisible. Black people are often more than abundantly blessed with suburban largesse. But the good and growth toward self-directed fulfillment of black people and the larger good of our communities as a whole are both served when all in America have opportunity to develop and utilize their potential to the full.

The thrust of Black Power is toward freeing the latent power of Negroes to enrich the life of the whole nation. The demand for Black Power is a demand to participate as full-grown men in making all of America become what it should be. When America makes the rebuilding of its cities a first priority, so the churchmen held, "then will the cry for 'black power' become inaudible, for the framework in which all power in America operates would include the power and experience of black men as well as those of white men."

The Moralizing of Love

A brief portion of the churchmen's statement on Black Power was addressed to white churchmen. It began by questioning the emotional quality of the outcry of some white churchmen over the use of the term Black Power. It was because of the abuse of power under some forms of integration that Negroes were forced out of the white church years ago, the churchmen held, and that Negroes also find integration often unmeaningful today.

The white churches have far too often assumed that a kind of sentimental love must prevail between whites and Negroes. Their programs of an interracial nature have been more geared to interracial love of a vaguely spiritual quality than to interracial justice. A number of the churchmen who participated in the meeting at the Bethel Church were clergymen in predominantly white denominations. These clergymen were of one voice in their objections to a false kind of "integration" where all real power remains in the hands of white people. A few weeks after

the July meeting of the National Committee of Negro Churchmen, most of the Negro clergy contingent of one denomination
met by themselves and indicated their willingness to leave their
denomination as a group, unless their potential was more equitably utilized, without regard to the existing unspoken racial restrictions placed upon the Negro clergy.

The National Committee's statement asserted that, for honest
interracial interaction to take place, all people need power: "We
regard as sheer hypocrisy or as a blind and dangerous illusion
the view that opposes love to power. Love should be a controlling
element in power, but what love opposes is precisely the misuse
and abuse of power, not power itself. So long as white churchmen continue to moralize and misinterpret Christian love, so
long will justice continue to be subverted in this land."

Solidarity for the Negro Community

The largest portion of the statement by the National Committee of Negro Churchmen was addressed to Negro citizens.
Here the prevailing theme was that justice comes most surely
through group solidarity. It has been against the building of solidarity among black people that white Americans have worked
throughout the American Negro's history. Negroes have been
given the opportunities and the justice associated with freedom
only as individuals. While not pointed to specifically in the clergy
statement, there was the clear recognition that the Supreme
Court school desegregation case of 1954 was the classic legal expression of this basic American pattern. At a subsequent meeting
of the churchmen, the evident (although completely uninten-
tional) infamy of that decision was discussed. The effect of the
court decision was to underscore the American tradition of opening opportunity to Negroes almost one by one, and a guilty system
remained effectively inculpable.

"We must not apologize for the existence of . . . group power,
for we have been oppressed as a group, not as individuals," the

churchmen declared. "We will not find the way out of that oppression," they continued, "until both we and America accept
the need for Negro Americans as well as for Jews, Italians, Poles,
and white Anglo-Saxon Protestants, among others, to have and
to wield group power."

Negroes as a group, it was seen, were denied at Emancipation
the "40 acres and a mule"—the economic tools—necessary for
the attainment of the power of substantial place in American
life. So it continues today. Free land was given to whites and
withheld from Negroes. Negroes have had to beg, to place themselves for more than a century as supplicants before the generous but capricious wielders of white philanthropy. They must
now move, so the churchmen urged, from the old politics of
philanthropy to that of self-development in our cities. In this task,
and from a self-conscious position of some semblance of power,
Negroes must share with white Americans in the great task of
urban rehabilitation: "The future of America will belong to
neither white nor black unless all Americans work together at
the task of rebuilding our cities." The urgency of the pooling
of power resources in urban rebuilding was underscored: "We
must organize not only among ourselves but with other groups
in order that we can, together, gain power sufficient to change
this nation's sense of what is *now* important and what must be
done *now*. We must work with the remainder of the nation to
organize whole cities for the task of making the rebuilding of our
cities first priority in the use of our resources. This is more important than who gets to the moon first or the war in Vietnam."

The potential power of Negroes, who make up 10% of the
population, was made clear. Negroes must first develop group
solidarity *as Negroes* and then establish effective alliances in the
cities. Negro groups of all descriptions were called upon to unite
for social change. Negroes were reminded of the need for reconciliation to themselves as persons and as an historical group: "This
means we must find our way to a new self image in which we can
feel a normal sense of pride in self—including our variety of

skin color and the manifold textures of our hair. As long as we
are filled with hatred for ourselves, we will be unable to respect
others."

The churchmen reserved their most judgmental words for
themselves, declaring that the Negro church has too often set
forth *"an other worldly* conception of God's power." They
pledged themselves to right in both word and deed this distortion
of reality which must be placed at their own feet.

The Mediators of Truth

For the press, in what was later seen to be an ironic way, were
reserved the words of greatest praise. The churchmen hailed the
role of the national news agencies during the southern demonstrations for civil rights. They asked for their continuing involvement in bringing before the public all sides of racial issues in the
North. The statement concluded with these words to the communications industry: "We desire to use our limited influence to
help relate you to the variety of experience in the Negro community so that limited controversies are not blown up into the
final truth about us. The fate of this country is, to no small extent,
dependent upon how you interpret the crisis upon us, so that
human truth is disclosed and human needs are met."

At the conclusion of the day's conference, photographers and
reporters met with representatives of the National Committee of
Negro Churchmen. The spokesmen for the group emphasized
how greatly the churchmen deplored the one-sidedness of the communications' coverage of the issue of Black Power. They expressed the hope that the national news agencies would not continue to report matters relating to Black Power only in a negative
context. It was made clear to the press that the implications in the
concept of power for the good of the whole nation were to be
seen as perhaps *the great opportunity* before the nation today.

The results of the press conference were meager. In spite of
the advertisement of the statement in several large daily papers,

the notice given in news columns to the meeting of the churchmen, as well as to the actions of others, both white and Negro, in
support of the concept of Black Power, remained as slight as
before. Almost daily the public was reminded, from early summer 1966 through the period of the year's November elections,
of Black Power almost wholly in terms of denigration.

The meeting on July 22, 1966, at the Bethel Methodist Episcopal Church in Harlem will be remembered, in spite of its little
immediate public notice, as enduringly significant for several
reasons.

It marked, for one thing, the beginning of a new form of
solidarity and communication within the Negro community.
When the meeting was about to be adjourned at approximately
4:30 in the afternoon, the public statement from the meeting
had not been quite finished. Upon one unanimous vote, the
churchmen agreed to commit themselves to the final statement
which a small, but representative, committee was to finish hours
after their adjournment. After the public release of the forthright
statement, the signatories remained in agreement.

The National Committee of Negro Churchmen, as an open-
ended group, promises to be the nucleus for the building of a
network of Negro leadership development throughout the country. The basic emphasis of the group is the need for the coalescence of Negro brain power and leadership potential so that the
unique insights of black Americans may be utilized for the whole
nation's good. This can best be done in the atmosphere of
mutual supportiveness and interchange among those whose common experience in America has affected their lives in common
ways. Negro thinkers have routinely complained that in a white
man's world they are accustomed to thinking as white men would
have them do. What the nation needs is not more of the same,
but the unique and potentially enriching insights of those who
sit at the margin of the nation's life. From the vantage point of a
kind of dramatic distance—albeit enforced upon them—from

the center of American life, black men of training and articulateness may perhaps best develop saving answers for the ills of the nation's life. The efforts of the National Committee of Negro Churchmen thus mark the beginning of the end of the appeals of conscience to power. From a new place of latent corporate power come to life, the churchmen see the need and opportunity for utilizing their own candor and competence for the benefit of the nation's life.

The National Committee of Negro Churchmen is committed to the betterment of the nation by recalling it to truth, freedom and justice within the framework of an equitable extension of power that is tempered by compassion and a sense of common destiny. They recognize that their role is a prophetic one and therefore they will face an uphill climb. But so strongly do they believe in the power of their cause that their subsequent meetings have been marked by an infectious optimism long missing in the fellowship of black Americans. Their effort symbolizes the new stance of a growing new black leadership for urban America. It holds, as those will see who enter into the spirit of the pages which follow, the promise of heralding a new day not only for Negro Americans but for every area and element of our nation's life.

II

A National Necessity

No Novelty

The theme of Black Power, in spite of much recent publicity, is not new on the American scene. Nor is it likely to die out in the foreseeable future, regardless of the outcome of the current debate concerning the propriety of the term "Black Power."

"Black Power" has been a continuing refrain in the history of the American Negro. The slave uprisings, which were more frequent than historians often relate, continually reiterated the Black Power theme. It was the clarion call of the rebel John Brown and of the abolitionist Frederick Douglass. The sophisticated and angered W. E. B. DuBois and the militant visionary Marcus Garvey addressed themselves to the issue of the black man's cooperative strength and dignity; and A. Philip Randolph's Brotherhood of Sleeping Car Porters came together, held together and became a major lever in American political and economic life through a commitment to what militants today speak of as Black Power.

What precisely does "Black Power" mean? In the Negro churches, it has most often meant a kind of black solidarity in a holy war where in an imminent latter day the saints of light, who have witnessed the evil onslaughts of the powers of darkness, will receive their due reward. Howard Thurman in his recent

13

and perhaps his greatest book, *The Luminous Darkness,* speaks of the perception of his early youth that white humanity was beyond the pale of his morality. Such widespread feelings of the mystical uniqueness of the Negro have been the backdrop for the political thrusts which we identify most often as Black Power. In its first several decades of militancy, the National Association for the Advancement of Colored People could have been fairly identified with the alleged dissidents of today who speak of the critical force of the Negro's united strength.

Such an idea today is frequently criticized for being open to misunderstanding, and subject to individual interpretation, and therefore possibly misleading. Since Black Power speaks—as it has done over several centuries—to the Negro's recognition and aggressive assertion of his own fundamental sense of dignity, integrity and worth, it must have flexible implications; for no two individuals can perceive and assert their own validity and place in precisely identical ways. The belligerent by nature will tend to express his own sense of being and relationship in bellicose ways; the more temperate will tend to use more temperate means. Nonetheless, there may be real danger in a mass rallying to the theme of Black Power. The Negro people over the years have been encouraged by many means to suppress and sublimate their natural feelings of conflict and frustration. With a long-postponed and new-found freedom, the potential catharsis inherent in the current call to the banners of Black Power may be fraught with painful excess. Black Power is a logical and much-needed expression of the Negro's awakening to self-awareness, a sometimes awkward stretching of his arms and flexing of his muscles as he looks half-bewildered at his newly felt but as yet untested and unmeasured political and moral strength.

Are Negroes Ready for Black Power?

Interestingly, those who oppose the use of the term "Black Power" have often raised the objection that Negroes court annihilation once Black Power comes face to face with white power. Such a vision of the armed conflict of two opposing and ludicrously unequal camps represents both a misreading of the intent of those who espouse Black Power and a failure to understand the necessary dynamics of social and moral progress.

Ethnocentrism, or the consciousness of in-group solidarity, with a consequent sense of pride and power, is one of the strongest of human sentiments. The nature of an in-group or an ethnic community is defined by the culture of which the group is a part. The American culture has defined a number of ethnic groups, including notably the Jews, the Irish and the Scotch-Irish, who represent religious, national or a combination of religious and national groupings. All of these groups have intense pride in their own membership; and they express this in a variety of ways. There are several singular and significant differences in the circumstances of the role of Negroes as an ethnic group in American life. The Negro's ability to express his sense of pride has been circumscribed.

Perhaps nowhere has this been more flagrant than in the well-nigh completely successful attempts of the white community, with the encouragement and complicity of the nation's social scientists, to have the Negro forget that he is by and large a European–American Indian–black African hybrid. The Negro has been encouraged to forget that the ancestors whose name he bears were of British stock, and that the varying shades of color and different textures of hair among his people are a reflection of a variegated ethnic ancestry. In culture almost completely, and in race to a fairly considerable degree, the overwhelming majority of American Negroes are of a European background. Yet the Negro's sense of racial and cultural pride has been restricted to his supposed African origins in a veiled and uncertain past. Rare is the writer of an American textbook in sociology or history who attributes to the Negro anything other than pure African descent, except in the semiderogatory sense of illegitimacy (although illegitimacy is common to all family strains).

"Black Power," then, may be seen to be a form of ethnocentrism, albeit falling into a trap set by the historically racist-bound American culture with the complicity of social scientists who inevitably tend to operate, hopefully with some objectivity, within the accepted framework of the society of which they are a part.

The Negro's sense of pride is further blunted by the un-American assumption that the Negro's position of social and economic inferiority is immutable. The "last-hired-first-fired" concept here may be seen to be not the result of individual prejudice but the logical expression of a way of life which rejects the Negro's worth. The Negro himself has purchased stock in this endeavor. Partly by recoil in self-defense and partly by imposed design, the American Negro has eschewed social equality. No major civil rights leader, even today, espouses as a major plank in his platform social equality, at the very heart of which is the matter of intermarriage. Yet economic survival and advancement, as well as a sense of pride, depend in no small degree upon relationships of a blood and legal variety.

Negroes today are isolated not only from the jobs at the bottom of the ladder, but also from those at the top, so desperately needed to begin a closing of the economic gap. Admittedly this isolation stems from an absence of contacts. Whom one knows is for white Americans as important as what one knows. For Negro Americans, the failure to know economically successful people in those intimate and familial relationships which spell care and concern and mutual economic responsibility means no less than a growing isolation from the economic and social fruits of American life, which are theoretically their due inheritance.

The renewed impetus toward the concept of Black Power reflects the apparent readiness of many Negro Americans to implement their now hoarse and hackneyed and desperate cry of: "All! Here! Now!"

Are Negroes Willing to Be Aggressive?

A story is told of an advertisement for what was billed as the most unusual show on earth. The day finally came for the great performance, and an audience in curious expectancy was treated to a one-minute show of symbolic behavior. Twelve Negroes were simply tugging hard at a rope. When those who had come for the show demanded an explanation, the producer simply asked, "Where on earth have you ever seen twelve Negroes pulling together?"

What is true of the American Negro is true of all ethnic groups. Everyone is unique, and only at critical and measured points do corporate interests emerge. For the Negro this has been both bane and blessing. With the current controversy over the use of the term Black Power, a concensus is sought where no agreement need legitimately exist. The fact is that, in spite of the massive economic and social indications of the monumental failure of the American people to close the gap between Negroes and their white counterparts, many Negroes are content with the current drift and trend of things.

The willingness to speak to the affirmative implications of Black Power may be in a closely proportional relationship to one's conception of Negro progress. On this issue, Negroes are not, and doubtless will not be, agreed.

Negroes, like all Americans, are generally better off today than they were at the end of World War II. The awareness of this fact leads not only many Negroes typical of the "man in the street" but also a substantial portion of recognized Negro leadership to speak with apparent integrity of the "progress" and "gains" which Negroes are making. Yet the American economy generally has been growing by greater degrees than has the Negro's alleged "progress." This leads other Negroes of equal integrity to reject the term "progress" with as much disdain as that with which some have rejected the term Black Power.

It is a sad fact that, in spite of all of our efforts in the Negro's behalf in the recent past, his relative benefit from the American good life has not improved at the same time that his perceptions of his own worth and due inheritance have tremendously increased. Further, the current programs under the auspices of the Office of Economic Opportunity and the extensive efforts of private and civic agencies on behalf of Negro employment and upgrading are all aimed largely in the direction of lower echelon and "made-work" jobs. These serve a basic and absolutely necessary purpose of enabling Negroes to survive and of postponing the day of massive revolt. In our present circumstance, this is no mean purpose and must be given the fullest encouragement at every hand. Nonetheless, the utilization of significant numbers of the available qualified Negroes in positions of high economic value and extensive influence at policy-making levels in our business, educational and civic structure remains neglected in a way which may prove to have perilous proportions.

Meanwhile, there is a growing sense of polarization within the Negro community. On one hand are numbers of middle-class Negroes who have bettered their status and who are understandably under the illusion of general improvement because of the tangible and unmistakable reality of their own personal progress. On the other hand, however, are growing masses of the disinherited who believe themselves to be forgotten by their traditional leadership, and who may be ever more willing to spell out in word and deed the implications of Black Power in terms of the frustration and depth of deprivation which they see as their lot.

Some economists believe that the economic system which is traditional in our culture calls for a fluid reservoir of untapped resource at its base. If such a reservoir is needed, as may be assumed from its sustained existence, the rudimentary economic problem becomes a potentially explosive social problem when the group at the bottom is not heterogeneous—being almost entirely

of one ethnic group comprising both the well-trained and some
who should be there—all through social injustice. Such has been
and is the Negro's plight. Even with increased education, statis-
tically only a relatively small proportion of the economic gap is
closed. In most communities in America, it remains true that
only after most white unemployed find work are the Negro unemployed given basic consideration. Hence, in 1966 in our large
cities, the unemployment rate among Negroes between the ages
of 16 and 21 rose from 25% to 34% while the rates for white
youth in the same age category were going steadily down.

The differing lots of Negro Americans have thus brought
about differing attitudes toward the problems of the present and
the future. Human nature is not fundamentally altruistic when
it comes to sharing power. Altruism operates within the strict
limits of our keeping basically the things that we have. Thus,
it is the height of folly to hope that all aspiring and upwardly
mobile Negroes and members of the secure white community
will totally support the aims of those who perceive themselves
as the disinherited. The cry "Black Power!" says "My share!"
for some. For others, it gives the completely unfounded impres-
sion of threatening their accustomed, or, hopefully, increased,
abundance.

Can Black Power Really Work?

The question of the feasibility of the use of Black Power is
mainly a rhetorical one. Our perceptions of the relative threat
or advantage which others pose for us is always with us. Further,
power in terms of human dynamics cannot be calculated always
in terms of numbers, and this is especially true where morality
is perceived to lie at the heart of the matter.

It is not a matter of whether Negroes can express Black
Power, but that they must, in the sense that the Negro must assert
his own inherent sense of worth and being, as all who would

grow up into responsible selfhood must do. Several centuries of admittedly crippling segregation and discrimination have not left the American Negro unaffected. He has been limited by this evil process, and now he must stake his claim to the worth which for centuries he has been denied. He alone must express his new-found self-realization. No one may do this for him or with him. It is so with our children in our own households; it is true also with rising social groups.

What, then, is the white man's role? Here one may appropriate the famed analogy of Booker T. Washington in claiming that today all Americans—white and black—must be as one—like the hand—in all that pertains to the extension of the corporate national good life. But each group must be as separate as a finger of the hand in staking its claim in its own individual way to its own due dignity and worth. It is a changeless law of human life that each man must claim for himself the dignity of his own adulthood. Those who would deny to the Negro this privilege would consciously or unconsciously will for the Negro that he be less than he should be. What he would do for himself today has been the privilege of all other Americans since the "shot heard around the world." If the black man has any power in American life, it is Black Power; and so the term is simply descriptive of a contemporary and, it is hoped, a growing reality in American life. As the Negro's response to the term Black Power is mixed, so is that of the white community. Many applaud what they see as the Negro's coming at last into his own. Others who have been close to the American Negro—and who may find themselves in positions of worthy and much needed influence in our national and local civil rights groups—may understandably regret the current impetus toward Black Power. To carry the analogy of growth into adulthood further, the lament of the white liberal (and consequently of organizations in which he has significant control) is not unlike the lament of a foster parent who contemplates losing to adulthood the child to whom he has become ac-

customed to giving succor. In the movement toward Black
Power, the white liberal's reluctance must be understood and
appreciated therefore as the attitude of one who historically has
extended the hand of friendship and upon whose help, once the
dust of self-assertion has settled, the Negro must continue to
rely.

To what strategic ends—aside from eventual growth and increased self-respect—can the movement toward Black Power
lead? There are at least several.

1—*National Self-Interest.* The Negro's current restless and aggressive protest may well be only a relatively mild and presently
self-destructive beginning of a massive and irrational response to
the continued arbitrary isolation of the masses of the nation's
Negro poor from the economic mainstream of American life.
Either we develop all of the nation's human resources for their
full productive potential and then open opportunities for their
effective utilization for our mutual benefit, or we create liabilities
which become a sustained, unnecessary and geometrically increasing burden upon both this and succeeding generations.

In this light, the contemporary impetus toward Black Power
may be seen to be a restorative and conserving force in American life, calling America to save itself from the folly of a myopic
vision of what America in human terms is destined and called
to be.

2—*Urban Improvement.* The life of our cities needs to be re-
deemed. The Negro's often angered protest represents the claim
that social palliatives in our cities no longer apply and that new
and fundamentally creative answers must be found for the
sores which fester in the heart of our cities' life. Our urban
schools, with their contemporary racial unrest, remind us that
the basic planning and administration of any enterprise at every
level must be sensitive to, and representative of, the concerns
of those who are served. Schools with proprietors as removed
from their constituents as our urban systems tend now to be are

as potentially insidious as the urban system of absentee land-
lords. Answers to the Negro's anxious pleas for education of a
quality which is worthy of a free and humane society may provide much-needed handles for meeting the needs of all . . . both
black and white.

   3—*Marginal Insights.* The Negro's present protest calls attention to neglected dimensions of the meaning of democracy. Thrust
outside the center of American life, the Negro is in the unique
and enviable position of bringing new and saving perspectives
to basic issues in our national life. His pleas for an audience
before the bar of American good judgment have helped to extend the meaning of equality. Our religious and national heritage, as well as the persistent experience of family life, promotes
the equitable principle of taking from each as he is able and
providing for each as is his need. Those who are deprived
and crippled deserve our richest and best resources in enabling
them to progress toward standing alone. Can a truly democratic
society reach for less than this humane goal? By virtue of his
rich experience at the margin of American life, we must demand
of the American Negro that, through his fresh insights, he en-
noble as best he can the common inheritance to which we owe
allegiance. Here a uniquely Black Power may be seen to provide
rich resources for us all.

   4—*Changed Status.* Inevitably, a declaration of the Negro's
changed perception of his own position creates a changed racial
situation. Surely the new challenges arising from the change will
provide a better groundwork than before from which to achieve
true progress.

   New conditions and uncharted paths are always fraught with
peril. We cannot foretell what the result will be of the impetus
toward Black Power. But the assertion of human dignity and
worth—as we may learn from experience with our own sons and
daughters—while creating times of trial and tension, produces
much good and growth and gain.

It is in the confidence and hope that the days ahead may be entrusted with their own problems, that we build today the human aspect of our corporate life. It is in this context that we may come to see and accept as a creative necessity the current focus on Black Power.

III

The Creative Use of Black Power

There are growing numbers who believe that we should move quickly beyond a rhetorical justification of the issue of Black Power and begin a kind of dialogue in depth concerning its creative uses for American society as a whole.

It is abundantly clear to many Americans that power is basic to all human dynamics. The overwhelming majority of the Negro clergy—who represent the most authentic Negro sentiment and who are themselves the only long-standing symbols of some semblance of power in the Negro community—are of the opinion that the past powerlessness of the American Negro in the face of the abuse of white power has made of the Negro almost a race of beggars for what are their God-given rights. Even the ultra-conservative Barry Goldwater has been quick to recognize the fact that Negroes must have power if they are to become what both they and America would will with equity for every American. We must give thought, then, to how the unique potential of the American Negro may most effectively be used, not only for Negro racial self-determination and fulfillment, but for the much-needed national regeneration which inevitably must be a part of the Negro's coming into his own.

New Insights Needed

At practically every hand today, since the creation of what
so many unfortunately have come to see as the massive cure-all
of the Office of Economic Opportunity, all sorts of interests have
been proposing, developing and administering programs for the
ostensible benefit of the Negro poor. If the wide variety of such
programs alone possibly could be taken as a measure of the efficacy of their operation, we might readily utter a sigh of relief
that the millennium was about to come at last. Some apparently
responsible men, incidentally, have actually predicted the achieve-
ment of this state in the next five to ten years. A close look at
the facts will show that few, if any, of these efforts go further than
ameliorating some ills, rather than curing any of them, or eradi-
cating the sources of our rapidly growing problems.

In Newark, New Jersey, which is the most predominantly
Negro major city in the nation outside of Washington, D.C.,
there are more than fifty disparate enterprises representing attempts by business, industry, churches, social agencies, and civic
educational groups to end the poverty of the Negro. Not all of
these are funded directly by the Anti-Poverty program, but most
of them are. Some of the leaders of the local Anti-Poverty program suggest that to eliminate poverty effectively in the City of
Newark will require several times the amount now allocated for
local programs.

The dedication, sincerity, and determination of the highly
responsible and eminent people who run Newark's United Community Corporation, and of their counterparts throughout the
country, is impressive. Their work suggests that dedication, hard
work, and massive sums of money will fulfill the dreams of those
who wish poverty to be driven from the land. Yet, as one looks
at the kind of quiltwork of the anti-poverty efforts in many
of our cities, it is increasingly apparent that some new ingredient
must be added if we are to remove or even to contain the roots

of poverty. There are those who are fearful—and I am among them—that abundant goodwill is no substitute for creative insight born of sensitivity and racial self-interest. Besides money and goodwill, the special gifts and endowments of those who currently espouse positive and creative Black Power are urgently needed.

Those who are concerned with the creative use of Black Power must have more control over the nation's efforts at the elimination of poverty, particularly in the cities. At this juncture in American life, the abolition of poverty in our cities requires the insights of the black people who are concerned with more than simple survival through the development of marginal skills and made-work. Urban poverty elimination must have the resources of those who are the most determined to see the fulfillment of the due destiny of the black people of America. Good can come to America as a whole only in the same measure as it comes to its parts.

This purpose is basic to poverty elimination, especially as it applies to our cities. The poor of our cities are largely the Negro poor. By the creative use of Black Power, involving the administration and control by black men of urban anti-poverty programs, this purpose can be achieved with the depth and thoroughness which the nation requires. This must be clearly stated, in spite of the apparent dangers which it invokes in the minds of some who fear Black Power. That Negroes themselves will tend to be most sensitive to peculiarly Negro needs is not a racist assumption but a reasonable conclusion. It is obviously inefficient to utilize second-hand experts or experts representing those whose leadership has led to past failures in terms of Negro progress where experts familiar with the problem at first hand may be obtained.

A white culture which all admit has been historically racist bound, abused white power and kept the Negro in the bonds of physical slavery for more than 250 years. For another 100 years it has kept the Negro economically enslaved—through the workings of the white American freedom plan for black people, Negroes have been kept firmly entrenched at the bottom of the economic ladder through the years of their alleged legal emancipation. So effective has been the Negro isolation from the economic mainstream of American life that, in spite of recent substantial and impressive American commitments to better the nation through a change in the Negro's plight, Negroes have made no substantial relative economic gains since World War II.

While the economy has grown, and a few middle-class Negroes have escaped economic thralldom, overall the gap between white and non-white dollar income has remained unchanged. This is where white leadership and blind Negro followership has led. What is needed today for black freedom—and for America's growth and gain—is the increasing leadership or full partnership of black men in all areas of American life, but especially in the area of Negro economic improvement. *The nation as a whole must encourage the leadership of black people, utilizing the best minds of white and black men,* to develop new approaches that will break the deadening overall "no progress" lockstep that has doomed the Negro poor and many others in our vast urbanized areas to a seemingly permanent rendezvous with poverty.

White men of evident goodwill and those Negroes whose chief concern is to blend with the white American landscape must always have a secure and highly significant, but increasingly supportive, place in the leadership of black economic development. White leadership in Negro affairs has served the good and thoroughly gracious purpose of keeping the Negro community alive to the point where Negroes might take leadership *for themselves, as have all other ethnic groups.* We must appreciate and be grateful for this fact. Now, however, the black man's progress and that of American economic development as a whole—will best be served by those concerned specifically with the development of black freedom and opportunity by the creative use of new dimensions of power from the unique experiences and resultant insights of black men. Black Power, in this sense, may well be the single most powerful force for the economic and moral redemption of our cities and the nation.

Several further considerations must be noted in the same regard. Those who have been crippled by the spectre of a ceaseless cycle of poverty need to have before them ready and close-range symbols of success. If successful black men in the highest positions of trust and authority administer to their needs, the desperate and hopeless Negro poor may come most quickly to have cause for hope. Also, if Negroes are, as a group, overwhelmingly deprived, then any new well-paying jobs which Negroes can fill should be set aside for the priority needs of the Negro. Any program—whether public or private—which does not do much more than deal Negroes into bottom-of-the-ladder pursuits is not fundamentally oriented to the nation's good. For it is the very isolation of the Negro from the economic mainstream of America that is the source of the increasingly widespread urban unrest. There are large numbers of qualified Negroes who need large numbers of upper-middle-class-paying positions now denied them in both public and private concerns. This problem urgently requires solution. A third benefit of black leadership is black self-interest. Surely, if administered by those whose feet the shoes of poverty pinch the hardest, programs for the Negro's benefit will be more likely to accomplish re-creation or reconstruction rather than just relief and amelioration of needs.

Criteria for Programs

This leads to the question of what criteria we must use to determine which programs are in the best interests of the poor. Here we may see that it is only those programs directly and immediately enhancing what we know of as Black Power which will clear from the nation's face the ugly and disfiguring blemishes of poverty.

When we set out to help other people we may have one of

several motives in mind. We may have a genuine desire to ameliorate, to lessen the pain of the problems of the poor. Or we may
want to help people to change basic power relationships so that
they can effectively help themselves. These alternatives represent
two fundamentally different viewpoints which have existed side by
side—and often have become mixed—in American life. The first
point of view represents an idealism with aristocratic Stoic foundations, the second represents a democratic Christian-Hebrew
idealism.

Aristocracy, whether of race or of class, conceives of power
relationships in semi-immutable terms. But with a rather rigid
structure of power relationships, there is an almost religious responsibility to provide for the care, comfort, and well-being of
those who are less fortunate. The Christian churches, as well as
private and public welfare agencies, operate perhaps most often
from such a fundamentally aristocratic assumption. To do otherwise would be to work against the *status quo,* which would be
revolutionary; and such agencies often are constitutionally committed to the conservation of order and the attendant prevailing
conceptions of the public good. Such an approach to the public
welfare goes by the name of *noblesse oblige* . . . and is part of
the real root of the massive problems facing all of us as a nation.

The impetus of a democratic Christian-Hebrew idealism, by
contrast, is toward the bringing of every human life to its due
and appointed flower and fulfillment, regardless of any change
in power relationships which may be involved. It assumes that
the public good—and the divine purpose—is achieved by the
fullest development and utilization of the totality of human potential. In such a construction, power relationships would be
fluid and dynamic. It dismisses the notion of any threat to the
security of the status quo; for human relationships are not conceived of in static terms. Life is seen to involve growth and
interchange.

The contrast here may be represented in a schematic form. I

have often made two columns, one headed "Relief" and the other "Rehabilitation." Then I have listed the attributes of a program to see which aspects fit under each column in this manner:

Relief (or Amelioration)	Rehabilitation (or Re-creation)

At times I have taken a look in this way at a day's activity and found, to my continuing dismay, that practically everything that I had done was far more on the side of relieving situations than of fundamentally changing circumstances or relationships in the direction of permanent good or rehabilitation. Those who are concerned about the development and creative use of Black Power must insist that all programs for the poor be basically re-creative. If they are designed principally to bring relief, no ready power for the poor to change their lot will be generated. Relief may help a man to survive, but relief alone—or even any so-called delayed power—will lock the Negro urban poor in at the deadening level of simple survival. This is neither in the interests of personal or racial fulfillment nor in the best interests of the fullest development and utilization of the human resources which the people of America represent.

We take as a case in point Project Head Start, which, in isolation, is seen almost universally to be good. Intrinsically, no one could quarrel with it, but when viewed from the point of view of the dynamics of urban or central city life, it may be seen to have more ameliorative aspects than might otherwise have been apparent. It may also appear, from this point of view, to be less important than other projects which, in the context of the peculiarities of urban life, would be more basically re-creative. Project Head Start is truly a magnificently conceived and ad-ministered, and much-needed, educational endeavor. What fol-

lows here is in spirit more a creative critique than a criticism of
a program so precious to the lives of many.

Project Head Start is designed to help Negro youngsters get
what its name implies, a head start in the educational process. It
has been an outstanding success in reaching this goal. No one
could quarrel with its worthy purpose or fail to see the need for
its extension. Yet the eventual pay-off, in terms of the basic reconstruction of urban life which these assisted youngsters may
eventually effect, will come in some twelve to twenty-five years
hence. Meanwhile new people with problems are forever coming
into our central cities both from suburban communities and from
rural areas elsewhere in the nation. One function of cities
throughout history has been to serve as havens of refuge for the
poor and the disinherited.

The rate of the migration to our urban centers of the poor, the
indigent aged, the diseased, the crippled, and the disinherited is
accelerating throughout the nation. Central cities offer more survival services of a specialized nature to meet particular needs
than do areas of lower population density. The adult needs in
our cities are immediate—and the most crucial. Thus beginning
with children for a solution to basic urban malaise, however
noble, is still but *noblesse oblige* when viewed in the context of
the nature and function of urban life. It is perhaps not incidental
that the most common contemporary characteristic of many
private agency and church-related programs of an ameliorative
nature is that they deal with children rather than adults. But
are not our downtrodden minorities, after all, like children?

The peculiar growth pattern of urban problems would seem
to suggest that any truly rehabilitative program—whether for
education or employment—must, of necessity, begin with the
adult environment. By starting with the adult environment, an
immediate change in power relationships is possible, and new
resources are built in without any further damaging postpone-
ment for the natural and indigenous development, undergirding,
and continuance of programs for the children of the poor. It

is important here to recognize that, when the poor are equipped to handle their own children, not only have we begun to develop Black Power, but we have started to place all of society on a self-supporting basis for the economic and moral good of all. But when others provide for their children's need, no increase of wanted Black Power, as a creative necessity in the life of the poor, is thereby effected.

Any program which gives power to the urban Negro will be re-creative in the context of urban needs. When, however, a program in any way postpones power for the powerless urban poor, such a program is at best ameliorative. Amelioration, we note, can always be used for good. Many sensitive observers on the social scene today would hold that any program which postpones the approaching day of mass violence in our city streets is good, and is not to be dismissed. Nonetheless, *we must come to judge any and all programs* designed for the fulfillment of American life *in terms of their ready and enduring promotion of equitable power relationships*.

Project Head Start, in this light, certainly should be encouraged and extended. However, it should be chiefly a supplement to a massive program geared to the effective reclamation and utilization of the resources of our adult urban poor. The plan which will lead to the elimination of poverty in our cities must have as a basic ingredient the ready and realistic development of the adult resources which we may fairly identify as Black Power.

Adult Priority Needs

The most reasonable means of achieving massive adult reclamation would, in other circumstance, be the most obvious. It is also the least expensive in both short- as well as long-range terms. The catch is that both the means and the ends involve an alteration of relationships of power.

If new mechanisms for the reclamation of the poor are de-

veloped, then the security of old systems of amelioration—and
those persons with power and position in them—would seem to
be threatened. Thus we may expect a kind of built-in opposition
to any significant change leading out of pauperism and into
power for our urban Negro masses.

I suggest, as one potentially effective re-creative instrument
readily available for urban social, civic, and economic reclamation
and development, a massive and authentic community college
system throughout the nation.

The major thrusts for such reclamation and development
should, on the basis of priority needs, be chiefly in our central
cities. The enterprise should be federally and state financed and
tuition free to all adults. It should be designed to meet the peculiar and growing educational needs of the idle Negro and white
adults in our central cities. It should not be largely the beginning
of traditional higher education, but only incidentally serve this
end. A community college, as we speak of it here, is not a junior
academic college that emphasizes youth education and teaches
subjects for a desired academic level of attainment, but a system
that teaches people in accordance with their peculiar economic
and social needs.

The classic function of community colleges has been to serve
the otherwise unmet educational needs of every adult in the
communities which they serve. In the development of such adult
education colleges in our cities there resides the greatest potential for massive educational reclamation, re-entry, retraining,
and the preparing for life as well as livelihood of the overwhelming majority of our nation's Negro and white adult community,
who otherwise will continue in increasing numbers to be burdens
on the more fortunate.

Creation of community colleges today is the most widespread,
urgent and immediate urban educational necessity. A rapidly
changing structure of social and economic life calls for the continual retraining in vocational and avocational skills and in the

arts basic to responsible and humane life in a free society of all of its adult population.

The poor who need retraining in livelihood techniques, who need basic functional literacy skills, who need to be brought again into the educational process, who need to be taught to add to the wealth of a free society, who need a vehicle through which to find a substantial measure of personal growth and fulfillment, who must be salvaged from the relief market, who need cultural enrichment and avocational training, who need the liberating sense of utility and purposefulness which an opening of wider educational horizons may produce—all of these are the kinds of people who could best be served by an urban community college enterprise.

What the Morrill Act of 1862 did for the white rural communities of the land, a Collegiate Extension Act of 1968 must do for the Negro and white poor of our cities today.

A little more than 100 years ago our national life was in the throes of transition, as we are today. Education of adults had been conceived of largely for an elite who could be trained in the "higher education" offered by or patterned after the famous Eastern colleges of Harvard, Princeton, and Yale. The nation, however, was moving into its agricultural western regions and there creating farms and building new communities. Its adult educational needs included the traditional classics, to be sure, but the most immediate need was for the teaching of agricultural and mechanical arts for the working classes. In 1862 the first Morrill Act was passed, providing for colleges to be set up in every state of the Union "in order to promote the liberal and practical education of the industrial classes in the several pursuits and professions in life." Known variously as agricultural and mechanical or land-grant colleges, these schools became the creative centers out of which economic, civic, and cultural progress was developed in the nation's areas of greatest need. Extension courses and experiment stations connected with these new schools made the impact of the agricultural and mechanical colleges felt in practically every rural household in the land. That they gave political power to the rural poor is an evident fact of their history.

Doubtless there were, at the time of the passage of the first Morrill Act, many sophisticated Easterners who felt that the "diluted" education of the masses, with its mixed diet of agricultural and liberal arts, represented a travesty of the educational enterprise. Yet the overwhelming sentiment of the nation was that continuing adult education designed to meet the peculiar and pressing needs of the day was a public good. So the land-grant colleges grew and flourished as they were encouraged by steady and more substantial federal and state assistance.

The new frontier for a new extensive national thrust in "popular" colleges is today in our cities. These are the areas of our greatest adult educational need. They represent growing trends throughout the nation.

In considering the unmet adult educational needs of our urban poor we must bear in mind two levels of need: needs arising largely from lack of adequate funds, and needs arising from a lack of comprehensiveness in previous educational designs. A community college system should meet the latter set of needs, those arising from inadequacies in former educational planning. However, it has been the national experience that the community college system inevitably catches the overflow from our four-year colleges in areas where four-year colleges can not meet anticipated enrollments. They have tended to become academically oriented to serve largely as the first two years of a four-year system. Or they have added two years and become four-year colleges themselves.

This trend toward higher education rather than massive reclamation of the adult urban poor has been perhaps most tragically seen in New York City. No community college has been located in the heart of Harlem; and the so-called community college in Brooklyn—an institution with a notable higher education-type academic program—is situated in the prestigious community of Brooklyn Heights.

Further, the so-called community colleges in New York—which are more nearly junior colleges in actuality—have been taken into the City College enterprise. Those responsible for the New York Community College system seem never to have intended it to serve as a massive reclamation instrument for those calling for training in potentially power-producing adult skills, although only in this way would they serve the overwhelming majority of their communities.

Traditional adult education courses without the added dignity and status of some kind of college credit are inadequate in a competitive and acquisitive environment. High schools are symbolic of teenage education. An adult educational milieu, to preserve an adult sense of maturity and self-respect, should be made available for both the continued education and the retraining of all adults.

The peculiar functions of an urban community college would suggest that a major hand in planning and administration of any prospective community college should be given to those of our major racial minority groups. To do otherwise would be to perpetuate the very incentive-blocking mechanisms which have made members of our major racial minority groups ask far too often: What is the use of trying? It would also overlook the need for a long-overdue breakthrough in utilizing some of the greatest unused potential available to the educational enterprise.

Traditional vocational education will not break the vicious cycle of stagnation which has kept the Negro, for example, economically isolated since World War II. Nor will more of it assist, as some would suggest, in offsetting the effects of automation.

What is needed is education in basic literacy and in a broad spectrum of skills, and a cooperative program between school and industry in a secure collegiate type of environment, but aimed at reclaiming every adult who is offering less to the common good than he should be. The rapid growth of automation suggests that adult educational reclamation and retraining efforts of a vocational nature stress broad techniques and disciplines rather than specific one-industry-oriented skills. Such an effort will call for a far greater involvement on the part of business and industry than has been anticipated in the past. Yet the effective redevelopment of our untapped adult urban resources must be done in an atmosphere of immediate rewards for motivation and survival, and sound learning geared to present realities and in substantial part to the future needs of an increasingly automated society.

Further, and perhaps most important, adult urban education must not be designed for those who are self-directed to want or seek further education. The education of our urban poor is in the local and national public's social, economic, and political self-interest. Those who, for the public good, need to be educated must be induced into the educational process. This means the creation of such new educational instruments and inducements as may effectively accomplish this public purpose for our cities and for the nation as a whole.

Today everyone in our society should have a minimum of fourteen grades of schooling; and the Department of Labor has been indicating for quite some time that our changing and increasingly technological economy will necessitate an average of four periods of retraining during an adult's thirty years of employability. Many of our existing two-year colleges, we have noted, have subverted their basic purpose to serve unmet adult needs and have become the first two years of a four-year program. This leaves our urban uneducated Negroes—and countless more whites—with little hope for the adult literacy and cultural enrichment outlets they so sorely need. It has been a growing national experience that vocational schools and adult high schools do not attract adults. High schools are for children. College is for adults. We shall not release a growing population of restless and potentially explosive urban poor from their vicious cycle of frustration until truly viable mechanisms for adult fulfillment are created. Private monies—as well as public—should be addressed to this end. Relief monies, and Manpower Defense Training Act and Office of Economic Opportunity funds can be used. The cost-benefit analysis for such programs favors such a creative educational thrust for our urban poor, who are, in increasing numbers, Negroes. In spite of many enabling leverages, new national legislation would need to be passed to give the due impetus to such a massive effort as is required.

The central, overriding economic fact regarding our Negro urban poor is that either they will be trained adequately for life and livelihood and then given opportunity for their due fulfillment, or they will become liabilities for which our white society must pay a major, geometrically increasing and never-ending relief and policing cost.

An imaginatively conceived urban college enterprise for most of the nation's cities must be oriented to the education of Negroes in no small measure if judged by the simple arbiter of unmet adult educational needs. Numerically, however, the largest proportion nation-wide will be for the white community. Here it is evident that by getting at the obvious needs of the Negro group we may devise handles for reaching the harder-to-pinpoint massive needs of the white poor in the nation. The basic facilities of such colleges always should be where the people are whom the institution is designed to serve. The difference between a community college and a traditional college has been said to be this: You go to a traditional two-year or four-year college; a community college comes to you.

A thrust toward the establishment of such a massive urban need in the minds of our communities and in the minds of our federal and state authorities is perhaps the first priority for the nation's good—and for the creative realignment of ethnic power.

What Can White People Do?

It is in answering the crucial and opportunity-laden question of what white people can do that Negroes have most often failed in the building of muscle into and in expressing the most glorious possibilities of Black Power.

A clue to the kind of answers which Negroes must in the future be quite careful to give rests in the fact that helpfulness on the part of whites in the past—largely in terms of amelioration—has not led to the Black Power so necessary to racial progress. Dr. Martin Luther King, in speaking before a recent local civil rights rally, emphasized the fact that over the past twenty years Negroes generally have been losing ground rather than making progress.

If Negroes perceive white people and white power as having been good and nice to them in the past, then perhaps they should overlook the abundant symptoms of the Negro's failure to achieve any greater destiny than he has. A local leader in a Negro community recently tongue-lashed a group of his colleagues by declaring that doubtless the clearest supporting evidence of an alleged Negro inferiority was to be found in the eager readiness of so many Negroes to buy at the drop of a hat any white man's agenda for Negro betterment!

In my own younger years, I used to believe that the inconsistencies between utterance and practice on the part of so many whites in racial matters were signs of an insidious and unacknowledged prejudice on their part. Experience has brought what may be a better judgment: It is simply not in the perceived self-interest of those in vested seats of power to think and act in terms that will alter their power relationship with those who do not have power. Thus unconsciously the whole weight of their perceived self-interest militates against basically creative thrusts of the mind and of the will, however much the heart may reach out for those who are less fortunate in that they have no power.

When a white person asks, "What can I [or we] do?" we must at the very first be quick to realize the possible differences of meaning which the question may have in the mind of the one who asks. It might be said that the windows of the heart looking out are often open where the doors to action by the will remain closed. People are reluctant to share power. Power is never freely set aside. It responds in terms of equitable adjustment only when confronted with implied or actual power.

Hence Negroes must never take the stance of humbly grateful beggars when seeking what at the very best can only be a part payment on interest of the debt which a white America owes for riding for three centuries without ever the thought of payment on the backs of black people of this land. Black Power, in terms of sweat and blood and pain of an awesome and callously inflicted daily degradation and the denial of basic rights, has built and sustained this land, which, in terms of unrepaid investment, is the black man's more than anyone else's.

What, then can white people do? Negroes can ask them at every hand not to do "kind" things, as in the past, but to remove the roadblocks which impede the fulfillment of the quality of Black Power which holds the best promise for America's coming into its greatest glory.

Certainly the removing of the defect of poverty from the American landscape and the development and utilization of the nation's fullest resources for the greatest good of all cannot come without the due fruition of Black Power as a part of the indispensable power of all who are America. Several practical tasks for the effective use and promotion of such Black Power as that of which we speak here may suffice at least to suggest the direction in which the combined efforts of white and black men must move for America's future good.

The black and white poor, along with most other adults today, must be given continuing education. All in our society need the growth- and fulfillment-producing values to be derived from a fresh continuing educational enterprise appropriate to the new needs occasioned by recent precipitous changes in our economic and cultural life. America must take firm claim to leadership in new adjustments to the late-20th-century revolution brought about by accelerated population mobility, the explosion of knowledge, automation, the evolution of new power relationships, longevity, and the concentration of people and problems in our cities. Statesmen and business leaders, churchmen, industrialists, housewives, labor and educational groups, young people, civic groups, the retired, and social planners—all these may seek to combine their energies and resources for a comprehensive coordinated and effective approach to literacy, livelihood, citizenship, and liberating skills so greatly needed by practically all segments of our society. This perhaps is the major educational and reclamation need for our day, and will do more than any other task to bring new hope to those who are disinherited and hopeless. This is basic, but will not be sufficient apart from the context of other approaches.

Negroes must be employed. The rebuilding of our cities should utilize not only the labor but perhaps more especially the planning and the management of Negroes on a far more extensive basis. Those who build in urban America or plan enterprises in it are under a special responsibility to involve in new ways and at higher levels those who are coming to be the major constituents of our cities. White people concerned with our cities or with the good of America can no longer look upon all or even most Negroes as fit for leftover or lower echelon work. Urban Negroes need new positions which reflect real power, and in the growing politics of our cities, if they are not afforded new power reasonably, they may soon appropriate it solely on irrational power grounds. The suburban housewife concerned with Negro betterment can perhaps help most by alerting her husband to the new needs of urban power participation in terms of employment of different kinds and degrees.

U.S. Department of Labor employment statistics, issued in September 1966, indicate the prevailing pattern in American life. At a great and needless expense to the whole nation black people are becoming worse off as the circumstances of whites relatively improve. Basic to the black plan both for black freedom and

American development as a whole is the need to employ Negroes in substantial numbers in significant positions now denied to them.

In the past and present, many white friends of black people have given in a kindly way a boost to a black person at the bottom of the ladder here and there. Helpfulness toward black young people is highly commendable. Equitable employment patterns at high levels especially need to be developed. Even the interests of whites in the massive employment of the black poor may be best served only when and if other black people are in seats of power not only to alleviate many obvious burdens, but also to serve as a symbol to those who are the victims of built-in despair. What is said concerning immediate employment must be said pointedly of every corporation and institution representing power from which black men have been excluded in any degree in every town and city in America.

White Americans can lessen the burdens of understandable black protest by paving the way and opening doors, not with the spirit of reluctance, hesitation or of "I'm doing a favor," but with aggressive concern for equity and the future development in justice and tranquility of our local communities and the nation. In this, at every step of the way, the best and most comprehensive participation, aid and advice of candid and competent black people should and must be sought.

Negroes must have mobility. Black men locked in a box are, at least temporarily, in a powerless position whether it be a neighborhood ghetto box or a job opportunity box. Those in our day who oppose the inherent right of their fellow Americans to enjoy the opportunities of all other Americans—whether in housing or in access to employment or to any relationships available to others—create for America the seeds of disruptive violence. Latent power that is boxed in is potentially explosive.

One of the most sure ways of effecting changes is to be "changed" ourselves. Many white people of apparent goodwill refuse to join in with apparent collusion against their neighbors in house buying or selling without recognizing that there are no alternatives besides apparent collusion with justice or implicit collusion with the injustice built up in our past. Change must come in one form or another. It is better that we choose the most constructive way. Those who are concerned with the future of America must make more pointed choices between the calculated and long-standing power of injustice or the perhaps less stable and less predictable growing power of freedom. No basically moral choice is easy; and with growing tension in America, power choices may be both more difficult and more urgent.

Negroes must have new places of influence. Increased influence may come through several possible approaches. It can come through more groups of Negroes with some semblance of power banding together to seek executive positions in corporations, bishoprics, deanships of cathedrals, superintendencies of schools, and high-management positions in banks, stores, investment houses, legal firms, civic and government agencies, and factories. Results may also be achieved by alert, sensitive and truly responsible businessmen and others who sit in the seats of power and recognize the need—for the sake of America's future—for a radically new power balance. The cooperative efforts of black and white executives, not for survival but for the sake of sharing power to increase power and benefits, can be one of the most creative thrusts in this sphere, again for the good of the nation—and individual self-interest.

In this regard black people need a new type of black-conceived community organization. The white-promoted plan for black community development, espoused recently by many religious groups throughout the land, implies a compromise on its face. It assumes that the needs of black people are the rock-bottom needs of those in depressed communities, when in fact a white America has left black people as a whole in a powerless position. It eliminates from its vision and further promotes the emasculation of black professionals, black craftsmen, and other competent citizens.

White Americans may take a major responsibility for the funding of programs of total organization of black people such as the one being contemplated in northern New Jersey. Here black politicians would be organized for more than sham political power, and black scholars would provide crucial insights and leadership in curing the growing ills of the poor and the powerless in our cities. Negroes *at every level* would be organized to create black unity, spawn black protest and to get around the past and present pattern of white intrusion and control in authentic black planning for substantial and realistic black influence. Further, the white community itself needs organization to be taught facts of life so often overlooked at the peril of all by a white-oriented press, frequently distorted by white social scientists and by white-controlled schools with a mind-set tied to the admittedly racist-bound mores of a white American culture.

White people and institutions, it must be said over and again, individually have not done the black man wrong. The villain is the white culture and society as a whole, of which they are an inextricable part.

Thoughtful white people thus will readily be open to accept black-engineered organization for black influence and for the creation of new power relationships which will reflect to the benefit of all. White people of genuine concern for America's future and for their part in it might take the initiative in demanding that such new approaches be made in their communities and elsewhere.

Negroes must have simple power. The churches and housewives of America may be on many grounds the most readily influential —if afforded answers by those concerned with the creative use of Black Power—in spawning a power reallocation. The white men of America who have power are associated for the most part with one or the other or with both such groups. Here may be the black man's best and least costly immediate lever for the enhancement and extension of Black Power. Our churches and housewives must labor not just to ameliorate problems, but to assist in the job of shifting power balances so that every human can carry his own weight and share in the responsibility for—and destiny of—America. They can both lobby and labor for staff upgrading and desegregation in every public and private agency with which they have relationships either in a primary or secondary way.

While there may be no ready excuse for the churches and housewives not to make an effort to encourage those who can determine policy changes, it should be clear that all must bear their part. Every American, in public and private concerns, must participate in both large ways and small in enabling all Americans to come to maturity and to genuinely help themselves. They may do this out of economic and civic self-interest, as working realistically to preserve their ordered and peaceable future and that of their institutions and of their children. Or they may work as builders of the late 20th century's distinctive contribution to America's dream. This latter task in our day—with the help of every agency in the land—may mean the fulfillment of America's truly great and glorious, and perhaps hitherto incompletely surveyed, potential through the equitable extension of power.

IV

Race Economics

A look at the need for Black Power from an economic point of view has a double advantage. It may bring significant light to the subject from a fresh point of view, and it may perhaps lead people more quickly to the crucial point of decision. So often it is true that, where men are slow to move on the basis of moral issues, economic elements may bring them to rather swift decisions.

How Far Have We Come?

For one thing, by looking at the Negro's relative power in its economic context we may gauge with vivid and compelling accuracy just how far we have come in our efforts to secure the blessings of the good life to our fellow Americans who are of Negro descent.

It has become almost a commonplace to suggest—and to believe—that Negroes in America since World War II have made the greatest strides in all of their long history in America toward their freedom, opportunity and inclusion in the mainstream of our

national life. Certainly during this period the civil rights movement has advanced at such a pace that its cause is no longer
espoused simply by the eccentric few but has become one of the
most respectable and hero-laden paths to prominence in America
today. Not only do the Republicans and the Democrats today
seek to outdo one another in terms of what they claim to be ac-
complishing for our nation's largest racial minority, but also white
segregationists are now softening their old line about the protection of southern womanhood and proclaiming ever more loudly
that it is they—far more than all other Americans—who have
the most authentic interest in the Negro's advancement into the
center of American life.

Such has been the apparent progress the American Negro has
made over the past two decades that churches, social agencies,
schools, businesses, labor unions, and social, professional, and
fraternal groups, far from evading any longer the issues of race
relations in their public and private deliberations and commitments, have all broken the conspiracy of silence and entered
boldly into the arena where the upgrading of the Negro's place
in American life is freely discussed and aggressively implemented.
At almost every hand such is the general picture that is presented
for our acceptance.

Yet when the so-called progress of the American Negro since
World War II is viewed in its economic context, a strangely and
perhaps frighteningly different kind of picture begins to appear.
It is the kind of picture which gives a certain sense of logic to the
increasing irrationality of the Negro's intensified and often angered protests. It also tends to put into a new kind of focus the
Negro's apparently cavalier abandonment of the so-called white
liberal, who once was seen to be his one secure ally, and to explain
his openness to the idea of the equitable extension of power.

We may examine a comparative statement of Negro and white
income in the Census Bureau's latest *Statistical Abstract of the
United States,* reproduced in Table 1.[1]

TABLE 1

Median Money Income of Families in Current Dollars, By Color of Head

1947 to 1963

YEAR	TOTAL	WHITE	NON-WHITE
1947	$3,031	$3,157	$1,164
1949	3,107	3,232	1,650
1950	3,319	3,445	1,869
1951	3,709	3,859	2,032
1952	3,890	4,114	2,338
1953	4,233	4,392	2,461
1954	4,173	4,339	2,410
1955	4,421	4,605	2,549
1956	4,783	4,993	2,628
1957	4,971	5,166	2,764
1958	5,087	5,300	2,711
1959	5,417	5,643	2,917
1960	5,620	5,835	3,233
1961	5,737	5,981	3,191
1962	5,956	6,237	3,330
1963	6,249	6,548	3,465

Source: *Statistical Abstract,* 1965, Table 472a.

The median family income here is most appropriate for our use in ascertaining the relative progress of the Negro, since the mean family income would be unduly skewed by a few high salaries of white people, and the mode is based merely on a head count.

It is apparent from the Census Bureau table that the American economy is growing. Total median income by families increased from $3,031 in 1947 to more than double that amount or to $6,249 in 1963. This means that, at least dollar-wise, all Americans tend to be making more money. This does not tell us whether or not these increased dollar amounts reflect increased buying power. Nor have we determined thus far whether the Negro's proportionate—though still quite little—share in the

nation's median family income has increased, as reflected in relative economic progress or a closing of the economic gap between
Negroes and whites over the post-World War II years.

When the Census Bureau chart which we have been considering is translated into ratios or percentage figures, a significant
story concerning the actualities of Negro progress begins to appear. The figures are in Table II.

TABLE II

Ratio of Median Money Income of Non-White Families to Median
Money Income of White Families, for 1947 and 1949 to 1964

1947	51.12%	1956	52.61%
1949	51.05%	1957	53.50%
1950	54.25%	1958	51.15%
1951	52.66%	1959	51.69%
1952	56.83%	1960	55.41%
1953	56.03%	1961	53.35%
1954	55.34%	1962	53.39%
1955	55.35%	1963	52.92%
		1964	55.98%

It is apparent that there is no clear statistical trend. This is, of
itself, of the utmost significance, since progress in American race
relations must be defined in terms of a clear trend toward a
closing of the gap between what Negroes actually have and their
goal of having a more nearly equitable share—circumstance by
circumstance—of the fruits of the American economy and good
life. That the American economy is growing and he is getting
not much less, perhaps, than in the past says to the Negro
principally one thing: He is still at least as much second class
in his citizenship and acceptance into the economic mainstream
of American life as ever.

From the ratios of median money income it is clear that the
highest post-World War II relative income period for Negroes
was in the early 1950s. While there was a low point in the

ratio of Negro to white income in the late 1950s, Negro proportionate income in the early 1960s was lower than in the early
1950s. This may suggest an overall relative worsening of the
Negro's position over a twelve-year period. To be in a position
to make any such inference when the American commitment
and philosophical thrust is toward an elimination of the statistical differences between Negro and white involvement and benefit levels in American life is more than sufficient evidence that
our plan for progress has been thwarted. It is this crucial message which has been heard acutely not only in Watts but also in
twenty other major big-city trouble spots recently identified by
federal officials.[2] It is this same message which is heard in
Bogalusa and Boston and in nearly every community in America
in which Negroes live.

The situation is complicated and intensified by the fact that
Negroes will not stand still and see opportunities and access to
liberating and enabling relationships due and denied to them
from their birth not only continually denied but bestowed upon
others who have been foreign to our heritage. True it is that
Negro Americans—like all Americans—are enjoying greater
benefits from a growing economy. We see Negroes daily in new
positions of wealth and of influence, but not in proportion to our
nation's growing wealth and to the greatly increasing opportunities for the extension of power and influence in the new structure
of corporate power being built both in our nation and our world.

Every American, no matter how unfortunate his condition,
may be better off than the workers in the rice fields of China.
Yet a man's lively sense of his own impoverishment and denial
must be measured chiefly in terms of what he perceives in relation to things that are close at hand. The American Negro *feels*
what the economic statistics clearly reveal: In his efforts toward
progress in relation to white America he has come up against a
stone wall upon which—in large characters which are to him
unmistakably and compellingly clear—he reads the word FRUS-
TRATION! Hence Watts . . . and what may yet lie beyond.

What Have We Been Doing?

Economics may do more than help to pinpoint progress. Economics may also provide a qualitative yardstick to measure the validity of the kinds of commitments which we have been making or which we may plan to make. Here we may ask two crucial questions: What are the economic implications of what we do in regard to race relations? And again, what are the race-relations implications of our nation's economic patterns? These questions may be treated as two sides of the same coin, for their answers are interrelated. A generalization toward which we have been building is that *the economic context of race relations may provide both a fresh understanding of our current situation and a clue to ways leading out of our dilemma.*

In business and government, in education and our social agencies, and in an increasing number of areas of our common life, there is the growing conviction that racial separation and disparity of involvement in American life are both wasteful of our nation's resources and unduly taxing on those who must pay for such waste. Hence such separation and disparity are seen to be immoral; that is, to be contrary to the *mores* or to that which symbolizes the common good.

Several illustrations here may suffice to underscore this point. Among city planners there have for quite some time been discussions as to the implications of the early Roosevelt era's restriction of Building and Loan Associations to home mortgaging. Such restrictions and facilitation as were prompted by the federal government have been seen in retrospect to have largely segregated the suburban communities of America, while leaving the central core of our cities to our major racial minority. The policy of the federal government was not seen to be based upon bias, but unfortunate consequences for the national good have been brought about.

What are these unfortunate consequences? And just what

measures are now being proposed to counteract them? The unfortunate consequences of Negro concentration in large urban areas include such things as:

(1)   Overcrowded, substandard housing, since new housing cannot be built today which would pay for itself and accommodate the poor.

(2)   As a consequence of the maintenance of large tracts of substandard housing, the land tax base of our cities tends to be reduced.

(3)   Meanwhile, there is an increased demand for services such as fire and police protection, welfare, penal and rehabilitation programs, new forms of education, added sanitation, public works, city planning and redevelopment, public transportation, parking facilities, etc.

(4)   Demoralization and frustration tend to become major factors in public life and in the community and personal life of those who are caught in our ghettos.

(5)   Unemployment rates rise, as the physical and psychological gap between employers and potential employees grows through a dispersal of industries to the suburbs and their lessening need for the services of the unskilled.

The implications of what we have been listing here are compounded by the fact that our metropolitan areas are fast becoming the centers around which our national life is focused. The central cities therefore need rejuvenation and rehabilitation, and these are the growing repositories for our nation's Negro poor.

It is estimated that, at the accelerating rate at which Negro migration to our cities has moved in the past decade. Negroes will constitute the majority inhabitants of at least the inner-city areas of most of our nation's major urban centers within ten or twenty years. Even some 1965 projections are said to be sufficiently off in 1966 as to make what was then projected for 1970 true in 1966.[3] Such is the case with Newark, which had a projected 1970 Negro population proportion of 46%, but which even now has a 60% Negro majority. Its school system's student body at this moment is more than 70% non-white.

What urban planners have tried to do in recent years is to use the same type of federal economic resources as helped facilitate our post-Roosevelt era residential segregation, to desegregate our central cities. With the intention of utilizing massive and calculated government aid, urban planners have been devising plans for the desegregation of our crucial central city areas. Their plans involve at heart the subsidizing of prime demand apartments or other dwelling units at such attractive rates that in the minds of prospective white real estate clients the issue of economy will by far take precedence over any feelings about the avoidance of Negroes. In much this kind of way urban planners hope to desegregate our inner cities, building attractive middle-income government-subsidized housing and providing unpublicized rent subsidies for poor Negro families to be housed comfortably among higher income groups who pay rents at a level adequate to cover building costs.

That the costs of basic improvement of the Negro's lot are less than policing and servicing costs in our Negro ghettos has prompted the federal government to initiate its rehabilitative programs through the Office of Economic Opportunity and has been a prime factor in recent legislation designed to improve our urban schools. The Demonstration Cities Project conceived by President Johnson also aims at using economic leverage to correct many of our race-relations-oriented problems in our cities. No current government programs, however, are realistically committed or geared to empowering the ghetto masses to grow into self-sufficiency through self-directed growth and creative change. Men and women—as well as children—come to hate the hand which too long feeds them. The radio news services carried not long ago a tragicomic story of an appeal by a group of Negro poor for loans from several foreign countries on the grounds that they wanted help to help themselves and that in

America they could only get a dole. People want to maintain their self-respect. When this is lost, little else of enduring value seems to remain.

Where Do We Go from Here?

One of the shibboleths that have been passed about concerning a resolution of the Negro's predicament as the holder of a substandard certificate of legal tender is that he has an inferior education. The obvious answer that is given is that the Negro will simply have to be more adequately educated. Then all his problems and disparities will fade away.

Table III tests this idea.

TABLE III

Ratio of Median Money Income of Non-White Families to Median Money Income of White Families Having the Same Number of Years of Education, March, 1965

Elementary School:	
Less than 8 years	65.91%
8 years	72.99%
High School:	
1 to 3 years	60.30%
4 years	69.06%
College:	
1 to 3 years	71.73%
4 years or more	87.59%

The table suggests several things: (1) Non-whites still earn substantially less than whites, even when they have the same amount of education. (2) That is generally true no matter how much education a non-white obtains. (3) A comparison of the 1965 ratio for non-white *vs.* white families as a whole (55.98% from the second table above) with the average of the six ratios in the above table (71.26%) indicates that only about one-fourth (the figure is actually 28.81%) of the disparity between

non-white and white family incomes is due to the former's, on
the average, having less education, while the bulk of the disparity,
almost three-fourths, is due to other causes.

Education alone, then, is not the answer. Yet a word or two in
this regard may be in order. Increasingly the civil rights movement has been setting its sights upon the schools. It has made
the claim that both *de facto* segregated education (which is apparently inferior) and otherwise inadequate education (lack of
concern, failure to appreciate the real needs of students, etc.)
are the inheritance of those who attend schools in our Negro-
dominated urban areas. Even though education alone may not
be the answer to the Negro's separation from the mainstream of
the nation's economic life, it is still true that inferior education
will only compound the problem. To the extent that inadequate
education prevails in our ghettos, more emphasis must be placed
on education, not less. This emphasis should be as monumental
as is the task, with recognition all the while that, in answering as
we must the Negro students' obvious needs, we may also be providing for the hard-to-pinpoint needs for countless other non-
Negro students.

The civic and business groups located in our cities or having
influence in them should lead in working to bring about better
urban education. Such tasks as changing age-old school districts
into sensible entities and creating new formulas for support and
responsibility, as between the state and the nation, may prove to
be economically more useful than our traditional halo-laden lady-
bountiful ameliorative stopgap endeavors.

The central, overriding economic fact or principle regarding
our Negro urban poor is that, as we have already stated, if they are
not trained adequately for life and livelihood and then given
opportunity for their due fulfillment, they will become liabilities
for which our white society must pay a high and ever-increasing
relief and policing cost. A reasonable ultimate alternative to
provision of full training and full opportunity is genocide. Some
feel that—as genocide was possible with a white Christian Ger-

many when extremist feelings held the day—it will be possible in America when white myopia and white lethargy and unwillingness to make the most of American potential meet the deadly monster of a mass of millions of resentful, angry, and untutored Negro poor caught in a vicious cycle of illegitimacy and vice causing almost total demoralization and outrage.

Along with this overriding economic fact is the clear reality of a failure of past mechanisms for Negro progress in relation to what white people of comparable potential are seen to possess. Obviously new approaches are in order, and for this the best minds that we have should be put to work. In order to do this, several crucial adjustments in our thinking will have to be made. First, we have to cease thinking of American race relations, for one thing, as "taking care of itself" or of its problems as being increasingly resolved over a reasonable period of time. On the contrary, we are creating a monster within our midst, a people being alienated from the mainstream of American life, not by a deliberately malicious policy but by the sedation of ourselves into the feeling that things are not really as they are. No business, civic or religious enterprise which has the privilege of operating in America has with that privilege the right to conduct its affairs in any way which may create undue problems for the nation or for any of its communities. It has no inherent right to operate in such a fashion as to create a menace to the public safety, compound or aggravate public relief and social agency burdens, and endanger the institutions of the land. Yet by the adoption of unfair hiring and other policies which have effectively isolated our black urban masses, these purposes which are antithetical to our way of life have been unconsciously and steadfastly served.

Every agency in our land must be committed to the promotion of the public good. To do otherwise is to be un-American. Therefore, new policies must be adopted, and—far more important— the damaging effects of old policies must not be built in as a permanent liability. Equitable adjustments must be made immediately in employment and other practices to overcome the potential social and economic peril already created by past policies and practices not now perceived to be in the public interest. Such a purpose must be aggressively and forthrightly pursued by determined and creative leadership, both public and private. The establishment of mechanisms for this purpose must be a first order of business throughout the nation.

A second thing that we will need to do is to cease thinking of race relations as a nice and good thing, as one important national and local task—*among many others*—to do. American race relations today, like religion and basic ideologies historically, must have an absolute priority . . . or we are as a nation lost! Third, we must accept the need for developing the potential of every citizen for the eventual betterment of the lives of us all. The impetus of all that we have said thus far is in the hope that—in some way—progress in empowering for change may replace what amounts to a present state of stagnation or possible retrogression.

Is progress in American race relations possible? The economics of our current race relations point to the need for some new approach to progress. Such an approach must give to black Americans the power needed to enter into the mainstream of American economic life. The thrust toward Black Power suggests that Negroes themselves hold the key to their own future. The turning of the key, however, may call for the resources of all. Thus the massive placing of the resources of our nation as a whole and of all its communities on the side of empowering for creative change may open the door of hope.

V

Self-Development and Self-Respect

What is said here concerning self-development and self-respect is designed chiefly as an in-group discussion for black people. It may have significance for others who listen in on this family discussion, as well.

Perhaps the central concern of the current issue of Black Power —for the good of the Negro and for the larger good of this whole nation and of our world today—is the self-development and the growth into maturity of the black people of America.

Black people have been the sleeping giants of this land. Among all Americans, their power, insights and experience, potentially ready to enrich this nation, have been least developed. In words of cosmic import which speak to black people in uniquely immediate terms, "we have not yet become what we shall be."

The black people of America are this nation's most rich and ready asset—its greatest raw material—as once the unmined earth and its untouched forests, fields and rivers were. In former years this nation built its greatness upon the utilization, not unmixed with wastefulness, of the vast physical resources which had lain untapped. Today, the new frontier of this nation's destiny lies in the development and utilization to the full of its infinitely greater human resources. What greater and potentially more useful reservoir of undeveloped and unutilized human resource does this nation have than in the black people of this land?

The Need for Self-Development

The great difficulty which we have had in coming into our own in America has only, in these recent days of impetus toward Black Power, begun to be made plain. We have operated, for at least the last crucial period of thirty years, on the assumption that Negroes needed to be led into their wanted place of maturity in American life.

This assumption should perhaps have been seen to be fictitious on its face. It is simply naive to believe that any person or any group of people may grow into maturity save in terms of their own self-development. Human growth cannot be produced from without: it must always be developed from within. Thus, thanks to the undoubtedly divine accident of the current focus on Black Power, black boys and girls, and black men and women—long lulled into a feeling of functionlessness and little worth—are awaking to realize that only through self-development can they become the people of power and of majesty and of might which their bearing of the image of their Creator has destined them to be.

There is, on the part of the Negro, a manifest need for self-development. Yet, of recent years, we as black people have assumed that a slave mentality of dependence upon others, as we had in former years, was appropriate for the twentieth-century destiny to which we are called. This crippling dependence upon others has hung like an albatross on our necks. It has led us to the state of stagnation and bewildered consternation which we find, with a few notable exceptions, pervading the life of the black people of America today.

The experience of all rising ethnic groups in this our beloved land has been that each rising group in American life must do for itself that which no other group may do for it. Each rising group has had to devise, to engineer, and to control in its own way its own plan, however crude or inept it may seem to have been, for its own particular growth into freedom, into self-development, into self-sufficiency and into self-respect.

This path of self-development has been—since the well-known rejection by the American people in 1776 of the King George Plan for Colonial Development—the one and only truly American way. There has never been in the American experience a German-American plan for Jewish development. Nor has there been in the American experience a Polish plan for Italian development. Yet the black people of America have been led in these recent decades to believe that their due fulfillment and their appropriation of their due inheritance in America could come best, or even only, from a white American plan for black freedom. This is incongruous on its very face. The issue of Black Power for black people—and for the good of American life as a whole —speaks to the need for black people to move from the stance of humble and dependent and impotent beggars to the stature of men who will take again into their own hands, as all men must, the fashioning of their own destiny for their own growth into self-development and self-respect. Now herein precisely lies the singular difference between the impetus toward Black Power on the one hand and what we have known as the civil rights movement on the other.

While the civil rights movement has emphasized what black people have been due, the emphasis of black self-development is on what black people may give to America. The thrust of Black Power is toward national fulfillment through the utilization of the potentialities and latent gifts of all. Both Black Power and the civil rights movement must have their vital and necessary places. The civil rights movement has in its own invaluable way emphasized what the American Negro has been due as an American from the day of each black man's birth. Without the efforts of the civil rights movement, particularly over these past thirty and more

years, it would be difficult to speculate on where we, and this nation as a whole, might be. The civil rights movement, with its
interracial dialogue, needs to grow and to flourish. We must never
indulge in the vain luxury of criticizing what our leaders—with
the aid of others—have done for us in the past.

What we must do, however, for the days ahead in the light of
newly perceived conditions is to establish new and more realistic
priorities in terms of the business of self-development. While pushing and participating in the absolutely worthwhile interracial program in the field of civil rights, the black people of America ought
long ago to have been addressing themselves to the far more
basic business of the development by black people of black people for the growth into self-sufficiency and self-respect of black
people. This is the main and previously neglected business to
which we must address ourselves. It is to this top priority concern
of self-development that the issue of Black Power calls the black
people of America today.

In the past, we've needed help; and we have received it. But we
lacked even more the fundamental necessity of self-help, and self-
initiative. It is by this alone we as a people may grow into that
self-direction and self-sufficiency which is encumbent upon all
who would claim the respect due to responsible and mature men.
It is by black self-development that this nation may come most
fully into its own. The absence of black self-development has
taxed the resources of the nation and limited the national destiny.

Now what, exactly, do we mean by self-development? We
mean, for one thing, that we as black people must put behind us
the "Hand me something" philosophy. Some of us will remember
the hard years of the depression. In Philadelphia, we are told,
they sang a song which said that:
    "Jesus Christ will lead me and F.D.R. will feed me."
And they asked, "What need have we, then, to fear?" Now such
a philosophy, in part, may be said to be good for any time. But a
part of it also is appropriate only on a limited and temporary

basis. It is said that if you give a man a fish, you feed him for a day. But if you teach him to fish and then *let him fish in the stream,* you feed that man for a lifetime.

Black Power in terms of self-development means that we want to fish as all Americans should do together in the main stream of American life. It means that we must reject the assumption that long-term relief is a reasonable option for any man. This assumption must no longer be allowed. It is a minimum moral imperative for men to be thrust into and sustained in substantial jobs. At this point, we as black people must not equivocate. We must make it clear that long-term relief is weakening and damaging to all poor people, and especially so to us as a racial group. We must demand the abolition of its use in such a way. When people ask us about what substitute we would offer, we must tell them that this involves a second step, which we shall get to next. In principle, the welfare system presently is an effective curse upon the poor. Once this is clearly and unequivocally established, we may then address ourselves to the need to devise ways for human rehabilitation. This will call, understandably, for resourcefulness. Finding ways for bringing all America's human potential to its flower is a basic moral imperative for our nation and is a duty which must be met by all of us.

Black Power means black development into self-sufficiency for the good of Negroes and for the good of the whole nation. We want—as others must want—to replace the helping hand which now aids us with our *own* hand—to sustain ourselves and not be burdens on all others.

Black self-development means something more, as well. It means that we want to put into glorious use the latent resources that we have for devising new ways of bringing fulfillment to all of life. From our position of powerlessness we have learned that only through an immediate and equitable extension of power can the black and white poor of our land be transformed from crippling liabilities into tangible assets. Poverty will begin to be abated most effectively when the particular and precious insights of black people are used in devising anti-poverty efforts.

Black self-development also means that we as black people must take the initiative—using the brainpower and the other resources of all, under our own leadership—in building black unity, black pride and black self-confidence for the larger good of this whole nation. A strong, independent press oriented to the needs of black people will help us to achieve this.

Black people have much to give to America. But it is only as black people first have confidence, pride and self-respect that they can give to America the rich gifts which it needs and must demand of us.

Self-Respect and Respect by Others

Undoubtedly the most crucial part of black self-development is the building of black men's self-respect.

Of all Americans, the black people of this land are by far the most intensely loyal. No one has ever questioned this. We are the unique products of this our native land; and in every respect —for good *and* for ill—we have sought to emulate and to fulfill all that is American.

In this endeavor, we have even gone so far as to adopt the white American disdain for all that pertains to blackness. The sad fact is that in America black people have been taught that to be like other Americans they must come to hate themselves. And this we all too often do with tragic vengeance. Doubtless many Negroes decry Black Power because of a cultural perception of incongruity between "power" and "blackness." Negroes are culturally conditioned to see themselves as childlike, immature and powerless. But the Scriptures tell us that we must love God with all our hearts and our neighbors *as ourselves.* How can we love our neighbors when we do not love and respect ourselves?

An eminent young Negro psychiatrist, from whom we shall be hearing increasingly in the days ahead because of his aggressive professional advocacy of the philosophy of Black Power, reminds us of the therapeutic need for the development of black men's self-respect. He writes: "The Negro community's high rate of crimes of violence, illegitimacy and broken homes can be traced in part to the Negro's learned self-hatred as well as to his poverty." [1] He believes that the kind of so-called integration which white people have offered to the black community "may have negative effects upon the Negro and may undermine his obvious need for strong positive group identification."

No man can instill pride and self-respect in another man. The same is true with ethnic groups. Every ethnic group, like every family, devises means of instilling group pride. Each idealizes its past and glorifies its ventures. So must the black people of America do. Instead of hating ourselves—as any group which dwells on its weaknesses might do—we must accentuate the positive aspects of who and what we are. Every Negro in America must come to grow each day in self-esteem and self-respect. This must be encouraged at every hand for the good of ourselves and for the greater good of all.

Not long ago I looked a black man in the face. His complexion was darker than mine. His lips were thicker than mine. His nose was flatter and his hair had a tighter kink. I might add that he was a black man's man in that he stood up for black pride through black self-development and Black Power. And as I looked that black man in the face, I could only smile, for I realized that I was looking at one of the handsomest men on earth! We must have pride in ourselves.

When we look at black women who have dignity and a sense of pride in themselves, can there be any real doubt as to the superlative virtue of Black Power? A black man, who might have been any or all of us, recently said this: "When I was a child I was led to understand something of the nature of my heritage. I came to understand that from my relatively recent ancestral past the blood of black kings and princes flowed through my proud black veins. I knew also that the blood of proud Indian chieftains was mixed therewith. This to me was a source of undiluted pride. Then I came to know that in a more recent past the blood of white aristocracy, the very flower of white manhood, made its somewhat mixed contribution to the determinants of my life. This latter fact gave me, understandably, no greater sense of pride. But from my youth up," he concluded. "I have grown in the recognition that black men, and women and young people needed to appropriate the proud black heritage which is theirs, perhaps in a sense above all Americans, to have."

Negroes must, then, be proud of the variegated blackness which is theirs. When once we have come to have pride in what we are, and have been and must come to be, then—and only then—will others come to respect us for what we signify first and foremost to ourselves.

We hear all kinds of economic and political and psychological theories about the nature of racial prejudice. But the more I read and reflect upon them, the more I tend to believe that fundamentally they are straining at a relatively commonplace mechanism. When so-called racial prejudice is looked at in the context of Black Power as self-development, it may be explained in an elementary and far more creative way in terms of the dynamics of family life.

Look, for example, at the well-known story of the Prodigal Son. The brother in that classic story could not forgive an apparent blemish in his brother's life. Whether the defects we see in those close to us are imaginary or real, the family or in-group rejects with an irrational vengeance those who fail to measure up to the family's patterns or its agreed-upon purposes or goals.

In this light, the American black man's failure to stand securely by himself, however difficult the task, may provide sufficient explanation for his rejection by the American national family. In this sense, the black American may be perceived as a permanent and potentially significant part of the American household, with so-called racial prejudice being the family's intensive reaction to the failure of one whom they wish to uphold the basic and continuing family tradition of self-development. To carry the parable further, we may have squandered a generation's treasure of time seeking after the elusive fruits of some degree of integration when we had not first developed sufficient pride in what we are to integrate as equals.

We need to have pride in ourselves. No one may give this to us. It is a matter of self-development.

The Redemption of American Life

Self-development, as I have said, may bring about the fulfillment of American life through the nation's answer to the Negro's incessant pleas.

The Negro people of America want far more desperately than any other Americans for this nation to come into its own. This means that the black people of this land are, like the Jews of old, a people peculiarly elected to transmit and to perform no less than a sacred trust.

It is for us as black people to take the initiative in calling this nation as a whole to growth into maturity. The past and present apparent immaturity of the Negro is part and parcel of a wholesale national immaturity. Immaturity has begotten immaturity. Neither a nation nor a family may become what it should be without an equitable extension of relationships of power. Fail to encourage growth into self-sufficiency, and the family suffers as a whole. So it is with us.

We who are black people want this nation to grow up into the fulness of mature wisdom and power and might. This can come to the nation as a whole only as it comes to its each and every part.

It is for us who are black people to take the initiative in saving the nation of which we are an inextricable part. We must take the initiative to save the nation from the path of economic self-destruction, as it spirals its staggering costs for a kind of welfare system which we must reject in favor of far less costly and more fulfillment-laden efforts at genuine rehabilitation.

Black Power speaks—by its insistence upon equitable power relationships—to the precarious and perilous plight of those who are too powerful and to the needs of all in America of every color and every condition who are destined to become less than they should be by a debilitating absence of power.

In some sense of the word, all channels for the operation of cosmic purposes are woefully unworthy of their task. This is said in this instance of a young man whom we shall not name but who might be described as rash and wonderful, irratic and magnificent, as perhaps demagogue and perhaps also prophet and who in his own seemingly immature and yet undoubtedly brilliant way has raised for our generation an issue which may hold the key to the resolution of so many problems in almost every area of our corporate and personal life. If the devil himself had raised in these recent months the issue of *power,* it could hardly be less grace-laden for us and for our world.

Not long ago I sat with a group of men who to me were as great as they were serious and perplexed. They were alarmed at the recent turn of events, in which people long working together, apparently in unity for the good of all in America, had turned their backs or retreated in the area of civil rights. Some of these men spoke in terms of gloom and of dismay. We all listened attentively, and then one clergyman present suggested that there was at least one person in the room who did not accept the spirit of the conversation. He was asked the reason why. His answer came in a way that should give our hearts cause for rejoicing.

He said that for years he had hoped that somehow and in some way the issues in the area of civil rights and of race relations and of every form of inequity for any and all people could be made far more clear than they had been. People with so many mixed and different motives were working together for apparently good and noble purposes in an effectively neutralizing way. Yet there were no sharp and plain criteria for finding out just exactly where the battle lines could be clearly drawn. Then came the issue of power, and for him light came suddenly out of darkness. Those, he said, who worked for the immediate and equitable extension of power were on the side of a God who sought to be revealed in the here and now as a God of power, of majesty and of might. Those who would withhold or make light of the need for the equitable extension of power were, whatever their verbal protestations, fundamentally on the other side.

He went on to explain that whether the backlash grew or diminished, from the day of that revelation, it mattered very little. For to him, nothing short of the long-awaited day of the Lord had come, where the sheep might be separated from the goats. If those who are for more equitable power, he said, were only few in number, as they might appear at this hour to be, then with the battle lines clearly and unmistakably drawn we might—with the prophet Elisha—at last look up into the heavens and recognize as we see the host of heaven and the chariots of fire that "They that are with us are more than they who are against us."

We move on to one more brief story before we close. Joseph, in the classic biblical story, was sold by his brothers into Egyptian slavery. Several things happened which are suggestive of the black people's role in terms of both self-development and the moral and social development of this nation. Like Joseph, we as black people have been rejected and enslaved in various ways. In our rejected state, like Joseph we have developed resources which might well have a saving value for those who have rejected us. We have been pushed out to the margins of American life; and from our peculiar vantage point of a kind of dramatic distance we can see more clearly than other Americans what life is like down at the center of the stage. By many signs which need not be named, this nation, like Joseph's brethren who came to him in Egypt seeking succor, may be crying out at this time for the saving gifts which it is the destiny of black men alone at this crucial hour to give.

Doubtless the import of all that we have been saying here has begun in a way to be made plain. The task of self-development is our burden and ours alone as the central task, as the main business which is before us. This we must accept and aggressively and forthrightly implement not only for our needed self-respect but also for the respect and acceptance of others, which must inevitably follow upon our growth into self-esteem and into self-respect.

This nation needs us, as does our world. We must take our hats from our hands, and we must stand on our feet. The old, if we but open our eyes to see it, has passed away. The new day is at hand. We must put away childish things, and assume the proud demeanor of men.

VI

The Public Education Battleground

The theme of Black Power speaks to the need to develop the nation's undeveloped human resources. The greatest untapped and undeveloped human resources in the nation are represented by the Negro community. The basic public responsibility for the development of these latent resources now rests with the public schools.

It is clear that the task of fully developing Negro potential has not been accomplished so far. Negroes have by far the highest proportion of school dropouts, underachievers, unemployed and apparently unemployable of any ethnic group for whom statistics are kept. Over the past several decades our public schools, particularly those in our urban areas, have received increasing blame for this situation. Indeed, much of the focus of our growing urban unrest has been centered on the public schools, making the educational system in some cities a veritable battleground of inter-group conflict.

In Chicago, the controversy, doubtless the most extensive in the nation, has led to the early retirement of the highest paid school superintendent in the land. In Boston, bitterness has deepened year by year, as a succession of seemingly petty decisions by those controlling the schools has been seen to hurl contempt in

70

the face of the Negro community. In New York some local people in the Negro community have demanded control of their local educational facilities. The list could be extended to include unrest of varying levels of desperation in practically every major urban school system in America. In our concern for the growing conflicts with the schools, we must ask at least two basic questions: What are the roots of the problem? Where can we go from here?

Education for All?

Those in a ghetto-like confinement in our central cities have complained more and more since World War II that they are being shortchanged in the schools. They cite the traditional statistics of the increased number of dropouts, the low reading scores, the old facilities, the high teacher turnover rate, the overcrowded classrooms, the low aspiration level, and the high frequency of disciplinary problems, along with the growing sense of the utter futility of the educational enterprise as it relates to the needs of the masses of the black poor who reside in our central cities.

These problems have been laid at the doorsteps of those who plan for and administer the public schools, and the administrators have not been wholly insensitive to pleas for change and improvement. Everywhere in our urban schools we see some combination of new teacher-parent relations, preschool training, tutorial and remedial efforts, cultural enrichment experiments, curriculum revision, in-service training for teachers, back-to-school and work-study projects, summer study opportunities, Negro history teaching and foundation-sponsored programs for the advancement of educational excellence. Yet as these programs (still for the most part limited pilot projects) increase, dissatisfactions mount. In spite of the unparalleled pouring of federal and foundation monies into new endeavors and experimental approaches in our urban schools, the conflict with the schools shows little sign of abating.

Mounting problems are inevitable because of widespread failure to recognize that the major problems of our urban schools are not basically rooted in the life of the schools. Our major problems stem, in part at least, from the fact that since World War II the economic and technological conditions under which the schools must operate have radically changed. New or old answers to problems which no longer exist lead exactly nowhere. Thus experimentation has inevitably failed to end the conflicts in our urban schools. It is the altered circumstances facing education with which we must deal if we are to resolve the mounting difficulties.

Is there no end in view? Just what is the really troubling problem with our ghetto people or with the schools? A brief look at the development of the unrest in relation to the history of education reveals several clues to the answer to at least the latter question.

The disturbance over and dissatisfaction with our urban schools noticeably increased after World War II. It was at this point that the impact of a war-created technological change began to be felt in the "back-to-normal" life of the nation. This change was of the utmost significance to the role of education in our society.

From the beginnings of our public school system throughout the nation, our schools prepared young people to live within the framework of a mixed farm and factory economy. The educational system was designed to fit people for life and livelihood within the then prevailing economy. Under such circumstances every pupil did not need a high school education, nor could most hope for higher education. The farms and factories needed hands with various levels of education, and the educational system was constructed to feed people into the economy at every level where they could be gainfully employed.

What happened after World War II was a radical shift toward a highly technological economy. The young dropout with his minimum of education was no longer economically useful. Being unemployed and now functionless, he became embarrassingly visible and served as the source of new problems because he had no responsible role in the nation's social and economic life. These youths included a preponderant proportion of Negroes.

Historically, Negroes have had the bottom-of-the-ladder jobs in the nation's economic system. After World War II it seemed possible that Negroes might be able at long last to move up the economic ladder and out of social and psychological isolation. At least this is the way things appeared for a brief period immediately preceding 1952 when Negro earnings came closer to those of whites than at any other ascertainable point in the nation's life.

Following 1952, however, postwar carry-over jobs no longer needed in the increasingly technological economy were eliminated, and Negroes were restricted in the unionized trades. Meanwhile, the urban schools continued to prepare young Negro students, as well as whites, for a no longer prevailing economic situation. This meant that Negroes still left school early, as in the past, but now for jobs which no longer existed. White youngsters were prepared for jobs which called for longer stays in school; and far larger proportions of white young people found jobs in the lower echelon trades.

Charges of racial prejudice have continually complicated the conflict with the schools. Doubtless there has been much conscious and unconscious prejudice—our racist-ridden culture makes hatred of or disdain for Negroes, even by Negroes themselves, an almost universal condition. Yet much of what looked like negative racism on the part of teachers in the urban schools was just the opposite. It was a kind of seemingly thoughtful care, concern and solicitation which prompted teachers of Negro pupils to encourage their pupils' studies only in areas where Negroes clearly would have opportunities to work or to succeed. The dynamics involved here hold true for white and Negro pupils alike. Why encourage a pupil to follow a course of study, or even to stay in school, when his studies would seem to lead

to nowhere? It is easy enough to understand the sense of solicitation behind the teachers' indirect vocational guidance. Yet our
understanding of the teachers' position does not lessen the social
consequences. This type of kindheartedness has effectively limited the opportunities before our Negro youth for several generations, and has considerably contributed to the plight of the
entire Negro community.

The pervasive influence of teachers on our social structure
must be clearly understood. Even where guidance counsellors
plan programs for young people (and the role of guidance
counsellors in social planning is staggeringly large!) it is the
classroom teachers who exert the most significant influence upon
the short- and long-term social shape of our communities.

Ideally, guidance counsellors work with teachers, administrators, parents, and pupils to determine what programs may
serve best the pupils' needs. However most counsellors, even in
the better staffed schools, are overworked. In the understaffed
and greatly overburdened central city schools, guidance coun-
selling is of necessity more often accomplished by decree than it
is by widely shared discussion. The guidance counsellor's role
is that of an official gate-keeper in the pathway to human resource development. He or she has absolute power over whether
a young person will be afforded even the basic opportunity to
widen his or her horizons. A terminal track or a nonacademic
course leads a young person to no less than a dead end. Clearly
more thinking must be done as to how best the schools' personal,
and ultimately social, planning can be accomplished.

The part that teachers play in this process of planning which
gives shape to our society is less direct than that of guidance
counsellors. Yet it is infinitely more pervasive. It is the teacher
who day by day must ride with or against the tide of frustration
and failure built into the life of ghetto homes. It is the classroom
teacher who often, in the most difficult pupil situations, offers
the only semblance of order in a pupil's personal world of chaos
and disorder. The classroom teacher must serve far too often as

disciplinarian in such a way as to compromise her task of teaching. The teacher also is a part of the community and reflects, consciously or unconsciously, the community's prevailing social attitudes toward those who live the inner city life.

The high mobility of inner city pupils further complicates the teacher's role. Following World War II, and precipitated to a considerable degree by the war itself, population mobility accelerated. Secure and steady long-term relationships between those who teach and those who learn are impossible in areas where schools have pupil turnover rates which exceed 100% in one year. Loss of stable relationships is damaging to adolescents, and is even more destructive to those in the primary grades.

The classroom teacher's role is crucial, yet well-nigh impossible. It is he or she who must take the children from where the home has left off to induct them into the life of the community and the nation. Pupils learn not so much according to the arbitrary limits suggested by aptitude tests as by how much their sense of inquiry into and excitement about life is turned on and then sustained. When a teacher in the central city schools is distracted from this task, or where prevailing but unspoken social attitudes decree, pupils are simply pushed through the little boxes which the classrooms come to represent in such circumstances. They learn little. The efficacy of general education and other terminal tracks—sadly for all—seems clear in these conditions. Society suffers from stunted lives and from the gross aggravation of having to bear geometrically increasing burdens representing the life and progeny of those who might otherwise have sustained themselves and then added to the good of all. Do not our teachers serve as social planners?

Self-Conscious Social Planning

Obviously there is a crucial need for more deliberate and consciously constructed social planning in conjunction with the public schools. Otherwise broad social burdens are improperly placed upon the schools, and our urban communities—as though by a conspiracy of silence—sow and nurture the seeds of a social dynamite which may prove too great a test for the nation.

The planning process in any circumstance must have a specific goal. In our urban communities, it is crucial that planning must be for the fullest possible development and utilization of the nation's human resources. For our black urban masses this means fostering growth into fulfillment both through a fitting educational experience and through access to relationships which provide real opportunities, not just unpromising ideals. This goal definition raises a number of questions, which will be dealt with below.

It should be stated here that what is essentially involved in our urban educational planning and development is the need for power for the powerless. The powerless poor—wherever they may be found in the nation—need, for the nation's good as well as for their own, to have their strengths perfected and added to the potential of the nation. They must share, as we shall see, in the definition of both means and ends, or both the means and ends will be compromised or subverted. Planning for total needs calls for total involvement. The needs of the poor and powerless in every community represent the basic and enduring needs of all in every community throughout the nation.

What, then, are the ingredients which must be a part of conscious social planning in conjunction with the public schools?

1—*Planning for urban education must be inter-disciplinary.* This foremost factor should be evident from the fact that the increasingly complex context of urban education calls for many and varied insights. The educational enterprise is not even chiefly an educator's task: it calls for the skills and insights of all who have a concern for and a stake in the molding of the nation's human resources.

Look at what we do when a serious "problem" arises in our schools. We call in a blue ribbon panel of experts. The panel encompasses ethnic and economic differences, and includes the most substantial representatives of business and the professions, some of the best minds from the most notable and accessible academic community and the best expertise from the field of education itself. This is what we do when we recognize that our schools are in serious trouble. The overlooked fact of the matter is that our urban schools are in constant and growing trouble. Yet our urban school boards throughout the land serve far too often either as the roost for politicians who might otherwise be cast aside or as the nesting ground from which the fledgling aspirant for public place launches his political career. Our schools are not the places for the game of politics. They are the potentially creative centers of the nation's life. In more immediate terms, the schools will be a continuing battleground for the poor and powerless who see in the schools the symbols and symptoms of their oppression—or they may provide the ground on which our cities begin to become what they should be. No less than blue ribbon panels in every community should operate the schools of the nation. This must begin with the distressed schools in our urban areas.

Elementary fairness for those who man the schools demands that no less than this be done. Unless our traditional public school educators want to take the blame continually for all the ills of society, planning for education in our cities—and elsewhere—must be inter-disciplinary. It must involve at every stage the whole range of professional and civic interest groups who broadly speaking are the real educators in our society. The demand by one local community for "control" of its local school facilities is simply symptomatic of a general need for wider representation, at significant levels, in the shaping and guidance of the educational enterprise.

Education in our cities needs to be reshaped for vastly new and increasingly changing circumstances. The best minds of the widest possible range of disciplines must be employed for this purpose. This must be true not only in policy making but also in the internal management of the schools. The superintendencies of the schools will in the future call more for the leadership of men with vision and with eclectic minds than for a self-defeating kind of bookkeeping which so clearly compromises the role of those who would give bold and imaginative direction to the educational process. In some cities new forms of continuing dialogue concerning broad problems relating to the schools are being developed. These include such interests as mental health, business and industry, city and regional planning, the churches, civil rights, school teaching and administration of various kinds and levels, libraries, museums, family and welfare services, federal and state agencies, local housing groups and officials, parents, tax reform, medicine, labor, and law.

The call for the development and utilization of the unused human resources of the nation inherent in the idea of Black Power necessitates, for the larger good of all, the working together of all potential power groups for the basic rebuilding of the nation's urban schools.

2—*Planning for urban education must be on an inter-group basis.* Such planning has to involve the whole community, at far greater depth and to a far greater extent than ever before, for several reasons. Because the context in which education takes place today is vastly altered—and will continually change—there is a greater need for interpretation. Inevitably the urgent necessity of economic mobility for the Negro community becomes a concern of the entire community, both black and white. Negroes must have an altered relationship economically within the total community, both black and white. Negroes must have this altered economic relationship within the total community if a holocaust —toward which it appears we are heading—is to be averted in the urban centers of the land. Past inequities must be overcome; and this paramount purpose cannot be achieved unless some new forms of constant communication and serious interchange of ideas are devised. Local communities and the entire nation must come to see the critical necessity, in their own self-interest, of investing in the creation of equitable economic opportunities and relationships for all. Patchwork and the implementation of simply a compassionate concern for others will not be enough to remove the marked cards which those in power have held in their hands for so long against the restless and increasingly resentful black masses who now overcrowd our urban centers. Only when those who now occupy the seats of power see that this is vital to their own self-interest will the monumental task be done.

Again, local nonprofessional citizens—the parents—need to be involved on an inter-group basis to create the kind of community solidarity which alone provides the power to deal with broad-based problems. Our communities as a whole must come to understand and collectively devise means of confronting the altered social, as well as economic, conditions which now prevail. Education as embodied in our schools cannot bear the blame for problems which are rooted in social change. Because Negro parents and pupils are hit the hardest in the changed situation in which the schools must function, a popular and unfortunate myth has grown. This is the belief that civil rights agitation is destroying the effectiveness of the schools. On the surface, it would seem this way. Hence, the greater urgency of local intergroup dialogue concerning the broad changes in which our schools and communities are involved.

The failures of our schools—saddled as they have been with monumental tasks and miniature resources—provide the immediate causes for the widespread dropout and underachievement rates, chiefly of Negro students. We must not cloud this fact. Our schools need more than to be improved: they must be redirected along lines which meet, not old needs, but the new needs of our vastly different world of today. But this tells only a portion of the story. It is like describing the visible portion of an iceberg, the great mass of which is below the surface of the sea. Where homes are different places from what they once were, where employment and re-employment patterns are markedly changed, where new attitudes on right and wrong on sickness and health are taking shape, where—at every hand—old functions have disappeared and new forms condition our common life: under such conditions as this, it is more than the spirit, direction and facilities of our schools whch must be refurbished and reshaped. Every institution in our society must reassess its task, if truly creative and mutually re-enforcing interplay and articulation are to be developed, and our society as a whole perform its total educative function.

3—*Planning for urban education today must be intensively intra-mural.* It cannot afford to be anything less. Certainly, we can say in swift self-defense and with sureness, we always take into consideration our teachers, our auxiliary staff, our principals, our guidance people and our deputy and supervisory personnel! But at what level? And upon what assumption, possibly outdated simply by the shattering thrust of new conditions?

The vital fact here is that every staff person in the educational enterprise, from superintendent to the custodial personnel, after decisions are "handed down," has a personal and irrevocable veto, once the door to his own classroom or office is shut.

It is an expensive matter to involve "line and staff" in what some call group dynamics, but to be "heard," to be effective where it counts, planning must be done in an atmosphere of community, where all are at least symbolically dealt into its processes. Only the surface of this particular need has been touched anywhere. Yet this aspect of the planning process must be considered, or all our other efforts will be for naught.

Intra-mural planning will foster more extensive and equitable utilization of the skills of minority-group staff members. It is odd, in a way, to hear white schoolmen speak of an absence of racial discrimination in the upgrading of Negro members of their staffs. Their position is understandable to some extent when we recognize that people do not readily equate cultural perceptions with biased feelings. Perhaps those who seek the more equitable upgrading of Negro staff personnel in the schools should speak of the inherently limiting or restrictive quality of cultural perceptions shared by all. This may get around the implication of de-

liberate viciousness in regard to the treatment of Negroes within
the education enterprise. To discriminate against Negroes has
been a cultural norm. To do otherwise would call for a deliberate
act of defiance of prevailing custom. Have those who are responsible for promotional examinations been deliberately and aggressively defiant of cultural perceptions and social norms? If they
have not been openly defiant, then the overt and latent racism
inherent in our culture has undoubtedly played its unhappy and
devastating part in the matter of staff upgrading.

If this were not true, then Negroes would doubtless be running
many of our urban school systems. Because of restrictions on
Negro professional and semiprofessional service in the past, until
less than a generation ago much of the flower of the Negro community tended to enter the teaching field, and these people became teachers in urban schools. The dynamics for professional
service in the white community have been otherwise. On its face,
it should be clear that the public education enterprise has many
underutilized resources. Intra-mural dialogue and planning can
at least help in overcoming inequities inherited in the mind-set of
our schools, as in all other institutions in our nation's life. Planning officers, possibly utilizing overlooked Negro personnel and
at the level of assistant or associate superintendents, should be
a part of every major urban school system's staff.

4—*Planning for urban education must be more closely coordinated on an inter-agency basis.* There just is no way out of the
present dilemma of the urban educational enterprise unless new
formulas for both guidance and financial assessments are developed by local, state and federal agencies and by foundations.
These should work together with more than cooperation—
that is, with the recognition of interdependence and shared
responsibilities.

It should be clearly recognized and plainly stated that when
the oppressed masses in our urban centers demand quality education to be paid for locally, they are asking for a near impossi-
bility. In the city of Newark, New Jersey, for example, every

good dollar spent for quality education represents for Newark nearly a dollar lost. The present pattern of population mobility in Greater Newark means that whenever people achieve a good education in Newark they leave the city for the suburbs. They take the benefits associated with their higher income and better education to the suburbs, and the places they vacate simply make room for more people who are poor and poorly trained. The poor and ill-educated tend to remain in Newark. Thus Newark today illustrates to an advanced degree the central city burdens and debilitations which will be the pattern of many other major cities in the nation. The city of Newark—with one-quarter of Greater Newark's total population—has ten times the number of families with incomes under $4,000 as all the rest of Greater Newark combined. The poverty proportion continues to mount each year. The newcomers bring few skills and represent more needs which must be met.

The people who add to Newark's burdens come from the suburbs, from Puerto Rico and from the rural South. Newark's overall Negro population proportion is 60%. Its Negro school enrollment represents more than 70% of the total school population. Yet the city of Newark must pay for educational problems created elsewhere; and when its people become educated, they leave, and Newark does not reap the long-term benefits. The educational tax burden on the people of Newark is excessive and self-defeating. It is like trying to make progress on a treadmill or pouring water into the sand.

What is happening in Newark is happening elsewhere throughout the nation. Clearly problems which are created by national or regional economic and social circumstances should be treated with national or regional funds. Every central city serves as a port of entry for those with problems generated elsewhere. Unless clearance to move into new areas is to be given by the receiving areas, then more than the local resources of the receiving communities should be more largely utilized to meet the extensive needs of newcomers to our central cities. The suburbs for the time being have effectively restricted much immigration. This pattern is un-American on its face. Yet it may be seen to be equally against the best of the American tradition to ask our already benighted and distressed central cities to bear the lion's share of fresh burdens which are generated elsewhere.

Those who are concerned with enduring answers to problems in our urban schools must work to create new formulas for massive and continuing federal and state aid. This should be coupled logically with new formulas for federal involvement. Perhaps most important, short-term pilot projects should be discouraged, simply because of their most potent and unintended result. Pilot projects serve in a self-defeating way to delay substantive commitments to move on a long-term basis in new directions. In our urgent times the glossing over of problems or their treatment with palliatives can only stockpile them for the day when our urban unrest breaks out into massive violence. The day for experimentation is—or should be—past. Bold new relationships on a regional, state and federal basis need to be devised.

The fact of growing population mobility will make it more and more evident that education is a national responsibility, as those who are taught move through their community of formal education into different communities of adult residence. The many growing suburban areas which find themselves on the verge of bankruptcy because of the excess of young families who are on the way up will find themselves at one with the urban centers in the need for other than local resources for the educational enterprise. All will readily come to recognize that the safety, security and steady development of suburban communities depend upon stable conditions in our central cities. Suburban home owners, businessmen and civic and religious leaders should be enlisted in the securing of new formulas for state and federal financing of central city education and of all education in areas of high mobility.

5—*Planning for urban education must set new goals in consonance with the altered conditions of our world.* A somewhat static society which is a free society has the steadying moorings of tradition. A dislocated society, such as exists, as we are most painfully aware, in our central cities, is cut loose to a large extent from its past. It is therefore dependent upon a broadly humane education for all of its citizens in a way which taxes the educational enterprise beyond all past imagining. We cannot be content to prepare the masses for livelihood and the elite for leadership. Our whole society must be infused with learning which will equip our citizens for the continual maintenance and development of a society of, by, and for free men. Only thus, in the final analysis, may we hope for our urban unrest to be fully overcome.

Herein precisely lies the built-in limitation of training programs to meet the needs of the inner city Negro poor. They do not empower for life as well as for livelihood. Although many of these training programs are well administered and do an apparently excellent job of meeting some immediate situations, they do not speak to basic needs. Nor do they address themselves to growing realities. Overwhelming numbers of black people do not need training for jobs. All they need is to become white for most of their alleged unemployability to be overcome.

The inherent thrust of Black Power is directed to growing and more pervasive needs of our whole society. Training programs not only miss the desired mark—and even aim far too short of it—in their preparation for bottom-of-the-ladder and made-work pursuits, when the Negro economic problem is immediate and equitable employment *at all levels*. These programs also—in a far more extensively tragic way—overlook the need in our whole society for humane education for life in a free society. This calls for enduring institutions which will work in far more substantial ways than training programs could ever hope to do in preparing all adults in the liberating arts which are necessary for us as a nation, if we are to continue to be free.

We cannot afford to have the majority of our future electorate ill prepared to make the critical judgments and choices which

make democracy workable. Both in public circles and in our
private lives there is an unfortunate but understandable and growing tendency to decide issues by means of force rather than by
reason. We see signs of it at every hand—in business, in labor,
in the civil rights movement, and in the law. The tendency cannot
be checked by force, whether physical or that of popular opinion.
It can only be overcome when we have both sufficient time and
sufficient tools to educate our urban masses—both young and
old and white and black—to live creatively under the new conditions of our common life. This alone calls for new resources far
beyond our present local powers to create.

Our education must cease to be remedial and become genera-
tive, however attractive remediation and so-called training monies
and programs may seem to be. Our education must begin at the
beginning and continue through the changing circumstances of
our individual and corporate life to help or enable every individual to realize his full productive potential and become what
he should be. The urban educational enterprise, it is suggested
here, must cease in its attempt to do the things of the past better
and focus its sights upon goals at once more massive and more
meaningful in the new situation which confronts us. Education
in the larger sense has not fulfilled its task until the last able-
bodied relief recipient has been productively set to work according to his reasonable potential and until all men's talents are developed and set free to enrich and brighten in the best way
humanly possible our communities and our world.

Planning instruments need to pervade our society, if basic
changes of the depth and extent needed by every segment in our
communities are to be achieved.

The Role of Foundations

This leads to a brief word about a possibly far more creative
and far less costly role for foundations than that which they now
play.

Foundations should aim at the production of self-perpetuating, self-sustaining and self-directed mechanisms for the empowering of people and communities in those tasks which people and communities ideally should do for and by themselves. With this in mind, private educational foundations might well devote their greatest resources to several specific areas of need.

There is the need to lobby for new regional, state and federal relationships with our urban educational enterprises. With massive and continuing federal support and with other long-term resources, there may be the promise of affecting the basic changes in facilities, teacher-training, planning and adult education, and in other services for human growth and fulfillment so greatly needed in our central city schools. The foundations can extend the benefit of their resources as they concentrate on facilitating the creation of the long-term public resources to perform clearly needed tasks.

There is a need to develop the overlooked and perhaps most promising resource available to the reconstruction of urban education. Our Negro scholars and academicians have both an experience and an investment in the dislocated urban community which cannot be paralleled anywhere. Seldom are the invaluable insights and skills of these men and women employed in the leadership and guidance roles in which they are so evidently needed and for which they are uniquely equipped.

The fact that they have had little voice in urban matters is understandable in many ways. They have no base of solidarity or united strength from which to articulate their concern for the use of their skills and insights. Thus urban planning goes on without the scholarly insights and tested wisdom of those most closely related in both feeling and experience to the condition which comprises the context of urban education. No graduate school of urban problem studies (which means, in effect, studies of the Negro problem) should reasonably be considered equipped to undertake its work without either the leadership or the primary involvement of black men of the greatest candor and competence.

Foundation initiative could serve a highly significant role in bringing solidarity and thus greater potential usefulness to the ranks of Negro scholars and practitioners concerned for the urban scene.

The need for solidarity is essential. Negro academicians as they participate in discussions by themselves will often talk with each other at first as though white people were monitoring their discussions. Then suddenly the moment of self-realization comes: they recognize that they do not have to speak or think in structured ways, and the open and clear honesty of these men reveals the richness of their unique experience. Clearly America needs new answers to its common problems. Foundations could play a significant role in spawning the kind of solidarity and communication among Negro scholars and thinkers which may produce the answers so sorely needed in many areas of the nation's life. They can also begin the more extensive utilization of these latent skills by insisting that urban programs which they fund be headed by, or involve in primary ways the insights and leadership of, black men of authentic ability and articulateness.

Foundations should undoubtedly place more of their resources into catalyzing long-term projects which aim at building muscle into the Negro community itself in its efforts at self-direction, self-sufficiency and self-determination. The educational development of the central cities calls for attractive vehicles of adult reclamation, such as the community-oriented collegiate-type educational enterprises previously discussed.

Foundations should encourage the development of these empowering adult education institutions *in the place of* debilitating and largely self-defeating preschool education. The adult environment in which young students live must be changed. Then the adults may undertake *and sustain* their own preschool and along-with-school study programs for their own children. Clearly foundations should work to empower communities to put first things first.

Those in the Negro community have the most to gain in imme-

diate terms from adult reclamation institutions. But every segment of our urban communities can have much to gain from this
crucially needed addition to the nation's instruments for human
resource development. Adult reclamation endeavors can move
black people from dependence and debilitation to independence
and to the role of benefactors of our society in many ways.

* * * * * * * *

The inherent thrust of Black Power is toward the development
and utilization to the full of the resources of black people. It is
a demand to be put into a position where the power and assets
of black people may enrich the lives of all. This is good for
America. It is a vital necessity for our cities. When our urban
schools begin to move boldly toward the fulfillment of this purpose, then we may confidently expect that the conflicts centered
in our urban schools will cease.

VII

Race-Related Problems

The present crisis in the field of civil rights reminds us that crisis is only one side of a coin. A Chinese character symbol for crisis is "danger-opportunity." This suggests to us that the present apparent crisis in race relations may actually be unexpected opportunity.

Being an action-oriented nation, we are always chafing at the bit, wanting to get on with the business, to get the show on the road. As the older "new breed" would say, we must hasten to "get with it." This has been no small part of our trouble in the area of race relations. We have failed to recognize that we must always know precisely where we want to go, if we are to prepare adequately for a journey. It is this kind of preparation that we have not been too careful about, particularly recently in race-related problem areas. We have operated far too much on the assumption that there was one race or civil rights problem to which we could address ourselves, largely by a wholesale massing of the troops. Hence the almost universal expedient of demonstrations or protests of one kind or another whenever the so-called race problem reared its ugly or perhaps potentially excitement-producing head.

The present crisis in race relations—where black people are

frustrated, at times to the point of fury, and where white people who have long been concerned with the welfare of their black brothers are perplexed and often deeply disenchanted—affords us the opportunity to reflect upon the nature of the problem or problems to which we would address ourselves. If we were to make a list of categories into which the so-called race problem might fit, we would probably recognize at a quick glance that the so-called race problem is of a variegated nature. It would be apparent that there are at least economic, educational, political, psychological and philosophical aspects to our race relations or civil rights concerns. At an even closer examination, we might come to see that what we have so long tended to think of as a single problem with many facets turns out actually to be a number of distinctly different problems—calling for different analyses and different solutions—but which are all related in specific ways to the matter of race. Again, in line with a repeated emphasis throughout this entire discussion, we may discover that a realistic grappling with race-related concerns may provide answers to more pervasive problems affecting far larger segments of our population as a whole. The impetus toward Black Power is toward national fulfillment through the use of the Negro's potential or power and initiative.

Economic Problems

We may begin to see something of the complexity of these race-related problems, for which we must develop more specialized and more highly refined resources in the future, by taking a brief look at several different aspects of race economics. Some so-called militant Black Power advocates have recently stressed a need—which is by no means new in the Negro community—for the development of cooperatives by and for black people. The need is stressed on several grounds. Black people are in the main poor. Hence cooperative buying may make many food, hardware, clothing, household and other items more readily accessible to the low-income Negro community. There has never been the hint of exclusion of non-black people from the economic benefits of mass buying by Negro-owned cooperatives. The more goods that are sold, the more profits for all. Indeed, the Negro poor have been credited in many areas with being the greatest potential benefactors of the white poor and oppressed. It has been the black poor people who have carried the massive burden of poverty pleas throughout America. Cooperative merchandising thus may come to provide a means of relating the poor and powerless to each other in new and unexpected power-producing ways.

The establishment of cooperatives involves organizational, educational and administrative problems. If cooperatives are to survive competition from individually owned businesses, the cooperatives movement will call for no little business ingenuity and for discipline in the Negro community. Inevitably also cooperatives will be related to politics because they will consciously become power-producing mechanisms.

The political aspects of the cooperatives movement go to the heart of American political life. Black people have no substantial stake in the capitalist or free enterprise system which is undergirded presently by our national political power. Indeed, it is the business structure of the nation which black people see as having denied them access to significant and power-producing roles in the nation's economic life. The "last-hired first-fired" concept has kept black people in economic isolation from the mainstream of the national life and has been the basic cause of Negro family disruption. It seems reasonable that the poor and those who also perceive themselves to be politically disinherited may seek new ways of expanding their livelihood possibilities at the same time that they develop new instruments for producing power. The Negro community since World War I has been encouraged to turn to cooperatives as a means of group self-interest and self-development. The expansion of credit unions among the Negro poor has been, in part at least, an answer to this challenge. The apparent success of cooperatives in the Scandinavian countries and the parallel success of the socialization of businesses in Great Britain (which has the greatest affinities of any nation with our own) give encouragement to the potential growth of cooperative efforts among the poor both here and elsewhere. The recent world-wide trend has been clearly away from the extension of the purely capitalist system. Undoubtedly the most strategic opportunity which our American capitalistic system has to preserve or strengthen itself lies in the possibility of providing the Negro community with both a substantial and an immediate stake in its operation at every level.

The Black Power thrust is toward the unity of black people for the good of the whole nation. It is a commonplace that Negroes of great potential are excluded from middle-management and other higher level positions simply on the basis of color. Middle-class-oriented Negroes and those trained to levels of high competence are being summoned to see their plight as being one with that of the Negro poor. They see as the first necessity not training, but *immediate* opportunity at every level for substantial numbers of competent Negroes, coupled with massive new training opportunities for others after them. The basic emphasis by industry and government upon new means of overcoming lack of training among the Negro community has come increasingly to be seen as a perhaps unconscious dodge to delay giving immediate and significant opportunities to *Negroes who are already more than adequately prepared* for jobs for which they would apply.

A common joke in the Negro community is that business people are looking for every black super Ph.D. they can find to replace white high school dropouts and others with not much more advanced skill or training. That picture is, obviously, overdrawn but the truth is evident that black people are largely dealt into the current free enterprise system only after the economic needs of non-black people are first substantially fulfilled. The movement toward Black Power implicitly raises for the American business community to answer the clear and simple questions as to whether black people are—in their view—a fundamental part of American life. If the free enterprise system is good for America, it must be good for all, for black and white, for rich and poor alike. America as a whole should be enriched by the bringing into focus of the issues here raised through the current dynamics of Black Power.

Whether the black cooperatives may be of permanent good for black people, and also pave the way for the adoption of a more effective and enduring price control system for the nation as a whole, remains to be seen. That the emphasis given to black cooperatives may move the nation to a crossroads affording radically different choices for the nation as a whole seems to be a realistic possibility. It is a race-related problem which the nation's economists, business leaders and the Negro masses must either collectively or separately decide.

Another economic problem, illustrative of the challenges facing specifically the Negro community, is to be found in public low-income housing. Basic investment in a community, and in the nation as a whole, encompasses home ownership. Renters tend to be less responsible than home owners for the protection or improvement of property values and for community upkeep and betterment of practically every kind. Black people are largely renters. Providing them with mass rental housing in our cities adds little to the revitalization of city life; it temporarily provides slum dwellers with a more sanitized form of existence.

The Black Power issue has served to spotlight the absence of power-producing mechanisms for the basic improvement of city life in the housing circumstances of the Negro masses. It has been clearly demonstrated that public housing costs more to operate under government management than it would under cooperative ownership by the tenants. In fact, the federal government has recognized that it would represent substantial savings to the

American taxpayer for new low-income public housing to be given outright to the prospective tenants immediately upon being built.

Why then should public management continue, if low-income housing management by public agencies is more costly than by condominium or cooperative ownership and management, and if the extension of home ownership is an essential ingredient in revitalizing central city life? Committees of public housing tenants, and of others concerned with government economies, taxpayer savings and urban rehabilitation, have been given encouragement, since the recent focus on Black Power, to accelerate efforts toward demanding condominium. To what extent these efforts will grow throughout the land or how effective their efforts may be remains to be seen.

That public housing among the Negro poor in our cities represents one of the most debilitating circumstances facing the Negro has been a long-standing and bitter complaint. Some equitable mechanisms in the direction of extending condominium undoubtedly should be worked out. The federal and municipal governments and the local housing authorities—like the public generally—would have much to gain from such a course. Housing authorities, freed from the fruitless burden of maintenance problems stemming from the absence of a sense of tenant pride and primary responsibility, could then address themselves to new, more creative and more exciting aspects of housing in our urban centers. This can, through the catalyzing effects of Black Power, benefit the life of the nation as a whole.

Educational Problems

In the area of education there are a number of discrete race-related problems. One of the crucial problems of education—not faced with the openness and honesty which the circumstances of our times demand—is that of the fundamentally conservative nature of the educational enterprise.

When John Dewey and others spoke so eloquently of education as a lever for change, they spoke of this as a possible new ideal. It was and is a radical idea. For the educational enterprise, as with every enduring public enterprise, is fundamentally conserving. These institutions, including our houses of worship, are dedicated to uphold and protect the prevailing conceptions of public order and public good. The American flag, even in places dedicated to the supreme honor of God, takes precedence. The nation "as is" represents "order"; and it is to the improvement of the public good *within the framework of order* that our public or civic institutions are committed. Our schools are a part of this order-preserving establishment.

It is both a physical and a sociological law that all change brings disorganization. Change tends to fracture or produce tension within public structures and public relationships. Thus our schools, like other public agencies, work for as creative as possible an adjustment within the framework of that which is. This fact is demonstrated in classic studies of implicit and direct vocational guidance efforts through our schools. Schools do not work effectively to promote a change in status or power relationships. To do so would, in fact, be subversive of the public order and create what would be perceived as new problems for the communities which our schools are designed to serve. This has a particularly adverse effect upon the Negro community, which, more than any other ethnic group in America, has been locked into the absence-of-opportunity box, and so needs almost precipitous massive mobility most urgently.

In the current public controversy in our urban centers between the Negro community and the public schools a larger public arena must be provided for any hope of seeing the issues whole. The schools may reasonably be credited with being open to as fair an amount of change as may be consistent with their basic commitment to order. What is at issue here is whether the traditional institutions for orderly adjustment are sufficient for the extent of change urgently needed by the Negro community for the good, safety, and welfare of the whole nation.

What we are experiencing at this juncture in our national life is a predictable collision between seemingly opposing forces that are basic to the fabric of our nation. On the one hand, we must have order and orderly change. On the other hand, the Negro community must have immediate and extensive change and a re-ordering of substantial power relationships. It is abundantly and frighteningly clear that Negroes have far too long—either for their good or for that of the nation—been effectively isolated economically, politically, psychologically and in every other possible way from acceptable production, benefit and other participation in American life. Hence, the seeds of the growing public explosion, the early signs of which are apparent in the black community's emerging confrontation with the nation's public schools.

A creative resolution of the seemingly impossible impasse can be effected. Here again, we may see how the catalyst of Black Power may serve as a creative instrument for the good of America as a whole. Fundamental to all adjustments are communication and perception of the depth of mutual interests. Dialogue is a basic ingredient in developing the atmosphere for change. Increasingly for many years to come the whole nation—and our world—will be faced with one constant which we may count upon: accelerating change, to varying degrees in every area of our common life. We shall simply move from crisis to crisis—with its utter wastefulness of both human and material resources—unless some new mechanisms are developed for dialogue and the strengthening of the perception of the mutuality of at least our public interests.

In every community in America many signs of waste and of alarm indicate that some such mechanism has been needed for a long time. The art of communication and disciplined dialogue can promote efficiency and effect seemingly impossible change. Our school systems, in our urban areas as elsewhere, should be employing both internally with their staff and externally with parents and citizens' groups some form of continuing and disciplined dialogue. This ingredient is needed in every area where common interests are involved. Just where should or might such dialogue take place? Earlier we stressed the need for the development of stable institutions for adult continuing education. Such institutions should be open ended to receive any and all adults. Here local business and industry would have many relationships. The concerns of the public common schools and of higher and technological education would overlap. Avocational interests would be brought into proximity with vocational concerns. The retired and the actively employed would be enrolled. Here, in brief, would be the long dreamed of and much discussed creative centers in our communities' life. Here, indeed, would be a natural meeting point for the kind of continuing community dialogue which brings about the readiness for adjustment even before concrete proposals for specific changes are devised. The central issue here is that new means of both intensive and extensive communication and education for a changing world must be devised, else the nation will be confronted with apparently insurmountable difficulties in the days ahead. Instruments can and must be devised for the preservation of order while at the same time facilitating the accelerated adjustments which will characterize a world of continuing and potentially exhilarating and fulfilling change.

Those who are concerned with both equity and order will be serving the interests of the nation in a further approach now being prepared to right the manifest inequity in the implementation of the 1954 Supreme Court school desegregation decision. School desegregation in an equitable way—for the fulfillment of avowed national ideals and for the economical operation of our nation's schools—was not even remotely accomplished. Indeed, tension has grown, as no reasonably effective approach to the massive problems involved was apparently made. A measure of compassion and of gloriously wise practicality would have seemed to dictate a "forthwith" decree for all segregated districts, allowing each district to apply for such extended relief as individual circumstances might require. In no small measure, the evident gross but unintended inequity of this case has served the good purpose of bringing to a head the key issue of power in the determination of goals and the devising of means thereto. It has aroused the determination of the Negro community to work for the betterment of the school enterprise as a whole, and in this larger context of community-wide and national self-interest to work for equitable enforcement of laws for the benefit of all. The schools for today and for the future need the total cooperative commitment of all. By relaxing citizen protest over the issue of integration, and by putting it into larger perspective, the fresh Black Power impetus among Negroes may bring about coordinated community efforts for the benefit of our schools in a way which has been impossible before this present hour. The ideal functioning of the schools, while bearing upon the Negro community's life in unique ways, is a broad concern which touches sensitively the lives of all. Betterment of schools is a race-related matter but is not at heart a racial problem.

The Welfare System

The problem of poverty goes hand in hand with the kind of extensive disinheritance which is the sad and increasingly ominous lot of the black masses who reside in our central cities.

Cities universally have served as repositories for the dispossessed. But there is no greater blemish upon the life of our affluent American Christian democratic society than our idled and disillusioned black urban masses. Their frustration is increasing to the point of fury. As their numbers grow, so their breathing space diminishes through overcrowdedness in slum dwellings. The demoralization which is the product of inflicted deprivation serves as the occasion for the imposition of further disabilities. Such are the overt or covert manifestations of what amounts to a black back-lash.

Immature personalities are quick to grasp at half-solutions.

Immaturity alone allows for the kind of racism which lies at the heart of American life. It stems from a feeling of such great insecurity and of threat to what we are that we must do physical or psychological violence to others. This is sadly true with our American culture, and especially so in its adoption of a welfare system which may yet provide the trigger for this nation's self-destruction. The welfare system, at its best, should have been looked upon as only a tentative approach to the social challenge and moral imperative of human development. Long-term welfare for any individual or group of individuals is both debilitating and degrading to the "benefitted" and is self-defeating economically, socially and morally for the so-called benefactor. Only through efforts at bringing life to its fullest flower may we be true to the democratic purpose of bringing the blessings of the good life to all. Those in the Hebrew-Christian tradition are under a further imperative to assist in the unfolding of that image of the deity which resides in unique ways in every man. Long-term relief as a continuing goal or option both subverts our nation's foundational commitment and desecrates a God-given religious purpose.

Thus the long-term welfare system in this nation must be abolished. It must be replaced by a system designed fundamentally to raise men to their feet, while only incidentally and temporarily providing relief from the pain of want. The preponderant weight of the creative genius of this nation should be directed toward the consummate purpose of human fulfillment. Only as fulfillment is brought to the life of every American can fulfillment come to the nation as a whole. The thrust of Black Power is toward the building in of power for sustenance and for the greater good of all in the life of every man. Welfare, as a long-term option, debilitates, produces powerlessness and diminishes the life of the nation in proportion to its retardation of individual lives.

There are several perils of staggering proportions built into the system which allows the option of long-term relief. It builds a growing mass of demoralized and impotent people who must drain the resources of the otherwise resourceful. It tends to create and sustain two Americas, an America of plenty, robbed of some of its fruits, and a world of waste where men, women and children are consigned to the lot of impotent and self-hating beggars. Surely this is unworthy of the potential greatness and glory of this land! The signs of unrest in our cities are unquestionably but the early warning signals of a growing division between the two Americas. A man taught to hate himself can do no less than grow in his hatred of others; and so with groups of men and subnations. On the other hand, it is reasonable to resent one's having to feed forever another man or other men who do not work, whose outrage gives rise to riots and whose resultant irresponsibility ruffles the wanted quiet and peaceableness of our communities throughout the land. Two nations, two Americas are being built; and they are set on a deadly collision course. The signs of impending disaster are evident at every hand; and yet we build in doom. Rehabilitation must replace relief.

The black poor and all who are concerned for America's future must reject the current system of long-term and power-denying relief. Rejection will not only avert the conflict toward which our course is now aggressively set: it can also sound the death knell of the entrenchment of obsolescent bureaucracy. The conservatives are right when they descry a growing bureaucratic trend which is self-perpetuating, and which is beyond both critical re-examination and curtailment. Such has been the case with some subsidy programs, which are seen to have become too cumbersome to unload or which are allegedly too politically perilous to roll back even for the nation's larger good. At some point a determined assault on useless or destructive functions in government must be made. There is no better point to begin than with our present far too highly involved and debilitating system of long-term relief.

There are those who believe that to establish a genuine system of human succor founded upon the commitment to rehabilitation, the old welfare system would need to be thoroughly replaced. The logistical problems of moving people horizontally into other positions in government are not beyond the resources of this nation. However equitably achieved, a new and determined commitment must be made to restore a kind of productiveness in government which benefits all the people, those whom government is designed to serve as well as those who serve. Thus the issue raised here by the impetus toward Black Power may serve this nation in unexpectedly crucial and powerful ways.

In this endeavor, yet another good purpose might be effected. The so-called private sector might stake and strengthen its rightful claim to share in both promoting and ordering the public good. The purpose of rehabilitating and sustaining those who might otherwise be established in long-term relief calls for the cooperative efforts of business and industry together with civic and public agencies. Government must not dominate life but provide ample frameworks within which the contributions of all areas of our corporate life can work equitably to promote and fulfill goals designed for the common good. Opportunity and access to enabling relationships cannot basically be provided by government. These must come from the so-called private sector, so long as the free-enterprise system remains. It is in the interests of the nation as a whole that all business and industry and groups for civic betterment must function. Thus either they must rise to the task of bringing fulfillment to America by providing equitably power-producing opportunities for all, or new ways of serving the larger public interests must be devised. The emphasis of those concerned with increasing the dignity and worth of black people (i.e., Black Power) is upon alerting every agency in American life to the need for rededication to our national fulfillment by providing opportunity and equity in every enterprise in American life to all in ways that serve our national purpose. Black Power asserts the determined purpose of black people to add their hitherto unused and potentially enriching gifts to the nation's common store.

Lack of training accounts, at best, for less than one-third of the disparity between the income of white and black Americans. The most significant factor in the economic, and therefore also social and psychological, isolation of the Negro from the mainstream of American life is the withholding of opportunity by those who control the private sector of our economic life. This is subversive activity. It undercuts and thwarts the common good. It works alone for national self-destruction. The most readily available lever for the development of a creative alliance and articulation of public and private resources for the public good— and therefore also for the growth and security of private enterprise and personal investments—lies in the wrestling with the rehabilitative problems of those who are needlessly poor.

The problem of full employment and its attendant problem— which will grow more urgent almost day by day—of the redefinition for an age of automation of the concepts of work and leisure are not race problems. They are race related, and their positive and thoughtful resolution will affect for good the life of every American. Here again, we may all have cause to be grateful to black people for raising the critical and only incidentally race-related issue of power as it bears upon our daily work.

Race Nationalism

Another pervasive race-related problem is raised by many of the younger advocates of Black Power. On the surface, it seems to deal with race nationalism or the separation of Negroes and whites. At heart, we may see that it is something infinitely more significant. It deals with one's sense of belonging in and to the environment in which one lives.

A not inconsiderable and apparently growing number of so-called "new breed" black Americans have come to believe that the major source of salvation for the black people of America lies not in vain efforts to make America a better place but in the development of black nationhood. By this they mean in specific terms the facilitation of the voluntary settlement of those black

Americans who wish to live apart in what may soon become the United Nations' mandated territory of Southwest Africa.

These young people explain that black people have no real investment in America, that America—despite its repeated protestations to the contrary—is indeed historically a racist-ridden white man's land. What men need most for basic human dignity, they assert, is the feeling of worth from their control of the land in and on which they live. Southwest Africa may well provide for black Americans, so these young people believe, a realistic hope of human dignity.

The issue raised here relates to more than a concern of new-breed Negroes. It involves a problem which lies close to the heart of urban life. The lot of growing numbers of the urban poor has much of the character of expatriation. The masses of the urban poor have neither land (or its substitutes in other forms of property) nor the long-term stable residence which makes for a sense of investment. They have little apparent stake in protecting or developing that little portion of the nation which is represented by the communities or neighborhoods in which they successively live. Their condition as sojourners tends to make of them users and not creators. Users are like expatriates: creators and maintainers belong.

The seemingly incomprehensible cry for nationhood, when seen in this light, takes on a meaning which speaks to a basic human need. Human life almost instinctively seems to seek for a place in the sun. Men want to belong. They want to be a secure part of that which is around them. Finding no part or place where they are, they may—if their motives are high—turn to the pilgrim spirit.

The new breed's call for nationhood thus may be seen as the cry of men who would be responsible and who yearn to be a basic creative part of the environment in which they are destined to live.

The call for nationhood by the black new breed may be heard as a summons for America to show all of its people in unmistakable ways that they belong to America's life . . . and that America belongs to them. There is room in America for all its people, and a manifest need for the potentialities of all. Through the agency of at least some of those who espouse Black Power we may be reminded of how every person in America must be provided with clear signs of his investment in both what is and what yet may be.

Organization for Development

The vain illusion of a newly emerging "integrated" society, which has meant many different things to many different people, has led the Negro community to de-emphasize the need for and value of the development of solidly Negro institutions for at least several decades.

That such an ethnic non-inclusive type of organization is both natural and American should be obvious. There are German-American organizations, and French-American, Anglo-American and almost every other type of hyphenated-American organization. The development of such organizations has provided both the means for ethnic group self-development and secure stepping stones from subcultures into the main cultural stream of the nation. The "stepping stones" have been there to use as one might wish. Integration of oneself into any aspect of life beyond one's own subculture has remained largely a matter of personal choice, for everyone except the Negro. For all hyphenated Americans, except for Negro-Americans, American life has been effectively desegregated. This is all that other Americans, as groups, could conceivably want. It includes the possibility of varying degrees of integration at various levels of the class structure at one's own initiative at any time. Negroes or their progeny, even if of a mixed marriage, can never be socially integrated in the traditional sense . . . for anyone with any trace of Negro ancestry is 100% Negro in society's eyes.

There have been problems attendant on the matter of the

Negro's subcultural organizations. In addition to social pressures and to personal preference to belong to a primary social or ethnic group, legal pressures have tended to replace the limitations once imposed by slavery. In a sense, the black people in America have never been fully free. They have been freed little by little, or restricted bit by bit, depending upon both white people's personal whims and the barometer of public expediency. Negroes have served as a kind of combination built-in safety valve and permanently available scapegoat to ease the pain to some degree of any or all of America's many ills. That the black people of America have been used or misused in this way is as fully understandable as it is reprehensible. The human tendency, unchecked, does not always incline toward justice. The limiting mechanism in this process must be the assertion by Negroes of the power of their own self-respect as individuals and as a group and the recognition on their part that they, as ingredients or elements basic to the good and wholeness of American life, cannot and must not be debased.

The black people of America, for the good of America, must today grow into a far greater solidarity than they have ever known. To suppose that this will result in the coalescence of white Americans into an opposing power bloc is farcical on its face. Negroes must come to recognize what numbers of white people, far exceeding the total numbers of the Negro people, have long known. Negroes as a group must come to know that their cause is a righteous cause. They will find in the white American communities great numbers of people who are bent upon the fulfillment of the claims of righteousness. Here we do not speak of a simple, tolerant or pious goodwill. Rather we speak of a prophetic concern for both the divine and the national purposes which, at this point in the black American's present plight, converge in a wonderfully strategic way for the good of all Americans.

Much of the newly emerging black leadership in America, undoubtedly including those that are the best paid, is comprised of black men of unsurpassed candor and unusual competence whom white Americans, bent on what can best be called righteousness, have helped to elevate to seats of influence and power. Black Power may lead to power coalescence, as we may well hope that it will. But the coalescence will be of both black and white people. For those in every segment of American life who want the dynamics of power, freedom, growth and interchange to bring the greatest possible fulfillment for America will see in the current focus on power for black people a long-needed and hoped-for opportunity for truly great things to come to pass.

Thoughtful white Americans, concerned for power equity, will foster black men's intuitions and insights to add their actual and potentially rich gifts to American life as a whole. Every effort must be made to convince every American that the immediate establishment of equitable power relationships for black people is in both the short- and long-range self-interest of every man, woman and child in America. It is only as white men see in Black Power a mirror of the abuse of white power that they are frightened. But look any self-respecting black man in the face, man to man, and discover that in his own stubborn sense of dignity there is nothing for America to fear. Indeed, Black Power is a proffered gift to bless the lives of one and all.

To achieve equitable power relationships Negroes must develop power fulcrums with which to deal equitably with those who represent the varied structures of power in American life. It is an increasing commonplace to see white men glow with pride and gratitude as they share in experiences where black men have at last participated with dignity and power, with courtesy, candor and command. America is enriched by every black man's growth into a sense of power and the nation is relieved from the debilitation due to carrying another burden on its back.

Black men must, then, organize themselves for their subculture's participation with power and righteousness in every aspect of the nation's life.

In recent years a number of efforts have been made at com-

munity organization among Negroes by people other than Negroes. They have been lauded as successful; and in many ways they
are. But limited successes which do not build in the pride of
self-initiative, however appropriate to the past, can no longer be
seen to be appropriate to the urgent and extensive needs and
circumstances of our present day. Negroes need massive organization for the urgent new purpose of self-development. This is a
task which calls for devices hitherto insufficiently developed. In
northeastern New Jersey a black plan entitled Community Organization for Development, or C.O.D., has been devised with
new assumptions in the area of community organization. Whether
the organization will come to be supported sufficiently to achieve
its purposes remains to be seen. Yet the approach adopted is a
valuable illustration.

The plan recognizes that the Negro community is not a geographical community, and that any organization for Negro development in a limited area serves only to further divide a benighted
community already nearly hopelessly fractured. Negro leadership
potential, Negro middle-class-oriented people, and Negro professionals must be brought into relationship with those who need
such leadership. When white-sponsored projects for Negro development fail, it is the Negro churches and the Negro middle-class
leaders who must put the pieces back together.

The C.O.D. plan calls for the organization of many hitherto
isolated segments of the black community—Negro businessmen, housewives, scholars, professionals, politicians, tradesmen,
the idled poor, etc., would all be organized in interrelated groups.
Existing groups of all descriptions would be brought together for a
coalescence of creative common potential. One day I met with a
representative of an exclusive Black Power elite which has met
quietly each week over several years patiently mapping a strategy
to revolutionize the civic and political life of the county in which
they reside. These men and one woman realized that they had
been effectively isolated from any highly developed black brain
trust or from dialogue with any group of white and black scholars,

whom they greatly needed at many points. The same day I met with representatives of political and social action groups, of a group called POOR, and of an educational and a religious group. These varied segments of the black community are growing in the realization that their corporate welfare is all of one piece: for the black community *as a whole* is isolated economically, politically and socially from the mainstream of American life. While they face many problems in common with many non-Negro Americans, there are many points where the common lot of the Negro calls for black solidarity. There is clearly a need for differentiation of the points where black people must work together with all in their communities to face broad basic problems, and those which affect the Negro adversely in particularly acute ways. There is also a need for Negroes to work unashamedly and unapologetically *as Negroes* for particular matters which uniquely relate to them. There must be broad new community-wide alignments of citizenry around concerns brought to a head by Black Power. There must be also black organization by black people for uniquely Negro concerns, especially so where a needed pride and self-development, so woefully lacking, must be built or fostered.

The C.O.D. plan calls for the organization of those in the white power elite, as members of the white power elite, to study and to grow into an understanding of how the expressed interests of Negro Americans are beneficial to them as individuals, as businessmen, as moral men, and as Americans. The interests and welfare of the black people of America must no longer be seen by any responsible Americans as a passing or sporadic personal, professional or civic concern. The welfare of the black people of America will increasingly be seen to bear upon the safety and security of our families and of our institutions either in positive ways of our own conscious making or negatively by unconscious means fostered by our own default. The C.O.D. plan calls for the organization of a white power elite with the aid of Negroes.

By far the greatest area of potentially productive white involvement in a race-related problem area is in converting and alerting white people themselves to the need for enabling every part of America to come to flower.

The C.O.D. plan includes the tri-city area of Greater Newark, Paterson and Jersey City. Because Northern New Jersey is an entity tied together by common tax burdens, politics, industrial needs, school services, social agencies, and expansion possibilities, the poor are related positively and negatively to the resources which they would command. In this same regard, no needless conflict is to be promoted with those from whom the Negro community seeks relief. There is the recognition that there are enough streams for black people to ford, without dodging existing bridges. Muscle will of necessity be used for real battles; there is no need on the Negro's part for fabricated struggle.

The C.O.D. plan recognizes that economically the Negro community cannot afford simple integration into business life at the lowest level. It will work for opportunities for older and experienced Negroes who may with profit for all be employed in high positions of trust and power and of commensurate income benefits. To give college scholarships to Negro youngsters and then employ no already available Negro professionals in one's firm postpones power for the Negro community and frustrates the urgency of our national purpose. Because of the particular urgency of high-level employment as well as of bottom-of-the-ladder opportunity, the C.O.D. plan calls for the leadership of an eminent Negro of sufficient national stature and command to have, as few Negroes possess, the force of reality with top business and industrial ownership.

The C.O.D. plan recognizes the imperative need to build permanence into its structure. Therefore the overwhelming majority of its personnel will consist of unpaid and part-time leaders who will work continually to sustain a black power fulcrum on their own. Only a very few leaders will be paid. Ideally any community organization should represent the zeal of its own constituents of a depth and determination for which one cannot pay. Organization should be an incidental or avocational commitment to which every responsible citizen should subscribe.

Thus the C.O.D. seeks to build in Black Power. It is not programmatically oriented. It seeks to coordinate existing organizations, spawn dialogue, and to foster the growth of organization where none exists. It will thus enable local people to become more deeply related, more extensively interrelated and more widely informed and empowered to build cooperatively—as time and circumstance may determine—for self-respect, self-sufficiency and for self-development. It will seek to encourage sufficient pride in black churches, businesses and other institutions that "reverse integration" may become a highly prized and worthy goal for any and all of white America.

It is evident that Negroes all over America must organize for the good of America. They must organize themselves and must take the initiative in the development of a new type of organization among the white power elite. The times in which we find ourselves are far too serious and the stakes are far too high for those interested in building up tolerance, goodwill and intergroup understanding to sit still in the chairmen's seats of any of our most vital concerns. Those who have the greatest immediate investment in black freedom must take the lead at this crucial hour. For the time being, there must be a realignment of tasks on the basis of a new estimate of priorities. Thoughtful and unself-seeking white people have been increasingly quick to point to this need. They have encouraged others who have led black people to step aside at least for the present time for the sake of the paramount need for Negro initiative in Negro self-development.

Black Power seeks for basic ethnic interchange, with the recognition that this can be achieved with wholesomeness only from the vantage point of equitable relationships of power and of respect for oneself and for others.

The Use of Terms

That there must be—and has been—give and take in American life must be clear to all. Yet the concern for Black Power raises in an eloquently helpful way the critical issue of the use of definitions in our intra-national interrelationships. To just what precisely does the *E Pluribus Unum* to which we give allegiance speak? Can it include the Negro?

We may see how American definitions and usage of terms adversely affects the Negro and thwarts his full entry into American life. In my own life I am a mixture of many things. Without give and take, without interplay across the irrational barriers of ethnic lines, all that is said in these pages could not be said. Aside from my wife and my brother, the brain trust to whom I turn most immediately for insights, for data and for encouragement is white. It comprises the staff associates with whom I work each day. These comrades sometimes drive me nearly insane, and yet without them at times I could not preserve my semblance of sanity. With each of my associates there are uniquely different relationships, all within the framework of understanding, of mutual supportiveness and respect. I am perhaps the most intimate staff confidant of several. There is a sense of mutuality and of apparent oneness. Could one ask for more?

Yet in spite of all appearances to the contrary, there is yet one crucial difference between my relationships with each of them and their relationships with each other. In the final analysis, they are all, by our national racial definitions, white. They marry white, as their marriage certificates declare; so have their parents and so, almost certainly, will their children. They all, within the very narrow options in any man's life, share in considerations for their future set by the limits of our peculiarly American racial definitions. Opportunities are open to them to some extent because my kind has been set apart as "something else." My restriction widens in some measure their every opportunity. In a thousand and one imperceptible yet real and effective ways their being depends upon my non-being. Doubtless they would will, and hope and pray that this might not be the case. But so it ever has been with them and with their kind. Is this always to be? We could go on to multiply examples of how restricted, modified or unreal our relationships—and those of others across the American definition of the color line—must tend to be because of our peculiarly American *use of terms*. What kind of authentic community and genuine interchange can there be between white Americans and those few who are defined as "something else?"

Sociologically there are greater and more significant differences among white men and among black men than there are between the so-called races. It is our definitions or use of terms which, in no small measure, gives rise to our divided state. Thus when white Americans speak of integration in our national life, it is often difficult to understand just what they mean. For white ethnic groups the tendency toward amalgamation has followed group or individual acceptance. In the American system of valuation, Germans, Italians, Poles, Jews—all in the final analysis are classified as white. Yet in France both black and white would be classified only as Frenchmen. There would be no use of divisive and self-defeating terminology. Our very keeping of statistics tends to create statistical differences. When Negro and white in America amalgamate, the issue from the resulting amalgam, by the American definition, is Negro. There is in America no such thing as half white, nor is there an omnibus listing as simply American by ancestry or by birth. Under such circumstances as these, for Negroes and white people to be encouraged to integrate socially without some overt or covert form of social restriction or control would in effect mean for white people, by our national definition, to will themselves gradually out of existence. For every child of mixed black and white parentage is by our present definition black. Our present national definition of who is a Negro allows for no reversal of the trend toward the elimination of the white "race" as it is now defined in America. Simple pride in

what one is would not tend to allow for white people, in the
present scheme of things, to do other than directly or indirectly
place some rather strict limits upon the dynamics of at least
some social forms of integration. Even the use of the term "integration" has presented a real bind because it allows Negro and
white social leaders to think of it as a possibility when, in reality,
it is impossible. Negro Americans are striving for desegregation in
or the right to access to schools, jobs, housing, etc. So-called integration, even if it were possible, could not be our immediate
goal if our main object is to make all men self-sustaining and
productive in a free-enterprise system. Yet access to enabling
relationships is related to economic progress.

The employment of our legal definitions of white and Negro
in our census and in other legal documents serves largely the purpose of division in our national life. It only calls attention to
supposedly significant differences and raises effective barriers to
communication, mutuality and the interchange between persons
who would feel that they are one. I raise this moral objection to
keeping racial statistics, knowing full well that much of this book
and many worthwhile projects for the good of all men would not
be possible without these needed facts. In short, it bothers me
deeply to know we need these statistics because we are largely
a racist nation. Thus those who preach or teach brotherhood
between whites and non-whites in America do so within what
are largely self-defeating limits. Morality here may be seen to be
inherently related to legal structures. False legalisms nullify the
best of personal intentions. Moral men cannot be moral simply
on an individualistic basis. They must critically examine and
judge all instruments of public policy. Those concerned with our
public commitment to make of America one people, under God,
indivisible, must work to replace a system which makes of America two nations and makes us other than we would will to be.
The problem assuredly goes even deeper than this. Yet our legal
words are powerful and inherently raise the threat of possible white American extinction. This is no mean thing. How-

ever superficial the force of words may seem to be, even this simple barrier serves to thwart our exploration of further limits which might be raised or done away with were this stubbornly effective barrier removed. Is this a problem for the courts? For the linguistic experts? For the Congress? Or for social custom? Is it a race problem? Or is it a race-related one?

The problem raised here also poses the question as to the possible limits of the use of the term Black Power. Does not the very emphasis upon self-awareness among black Americans tend to defeat the dynamics of nationality solidarity? Doubtless we must say unequivocally that power for all is both a good and necessary thing. Black Power here may be likened, in some degree and sense, to sex and religion, in that it has great possibilities for the public good, if not used in illicit ways. Black Power must be used to take us to the point of black self-development and pride and to the adding of black America's potential to America's common store. But Black Power, in spite of its basically positive nature, must not be used beyond the bounds within which it serves what may be seen as the divine purpose of human growth and brings fulfillment to our nation's life.

The current impetus toward Black Power thus may fundamentally serve the good of the nation as a whole in reminding us of the strict limits of all forms of power. The conscious use and articulation of Black Power must make white Americans painfully aware of the dangers of the long-standing unconscious and unexpressed abuse of power by white Americans even as it reminds Negroes of the utter degradation of powerlessness in the face of the unchallenged abuse of power. Doubtless, the issue of power should always have been consciously thought of and freely discussed. Yet this very purpose may be served now as Black Power brings into focus a kind of alienation between Americans which most people assuredly would not want and would doubtless pay any reasonable price to overcome. All terms, including Black Power along with our present definitions of what kinds of Americans we are, must be seen to have strict limits. Their good must always be gauged by the extent to which they serve the common good.

Race-related problems, it has been suggested here, are many and varied. They are open to different forms of analysis and to different methods of resolution. They affect the Negro in perhaps precise and painful ways. Yet the problems of the Negro community may best be seen in a larger perspective where they relate to the needs, and call for the resources, of all.

VIII

Black Leadership and American Goals

The thrust toward Black Power inevitably raises the question of the relationship of black leadership to the attainment of certain basic American goals. Has the leadership which has been given in race-related concerns achieved the fundamental goals for Negro Americans to which the nation has been committed for all Americans? To what extent has past leadership been effective in ostensibly Negro affairs or in problem areas relating uniquely to the Negro?

The questions posed here are significant because it seems increasingly clear that the only choice before us as a nation is between the continuation of such growing urban chaos and consternation as we are witnessing on the one hand and a genuine thrust toward the goal of empowering for and guaranteeing to all Americans a better life on the other hand. The words here—as elsewhere throughout this book—may seem at times ominous or pessimistic. But evidence is cited, and is daily confirmed in our news reports and in the growing tensions in our urban communities, which points to a mounting and disconcerting unrest. This alone should be sufficient to call us to a re-evaluation both of where we are headed and of the resources which we have been using for leadership. History is filled with illustrations of

116

how ignoring clear signs of disorder and distress almost universally precedes disaster. If the urgent case for grave concern
over our apparently worsening and perilous plight is overdrawn,
no harm will have been done in pricking the conscience of the
nation to improve what needs to be improved. If however, the
case presented for the gravity of the nation's predicament is both
sober and sound, it behooves us to reassess very quickly the relationship between the kinds of people whom we have chosen to
solve our problems and the nature of the problems themselves.

What we need is the immediate and extensive utilization of the
unique insights and leadership potential of black men and
women. This is another way of saying that the unused resources
and latent power of all must be used for the common good. This
must be done especially in all the broad problem areas on the
urban scene which, while substantially affecting all Americans,
touch in immediately critical ways the life of black Americans.

The Twists of Fate and Fortune

Negro Americans have had relatively little to say in the broad
decision-making processes in the nation's life. Even the life of
black America has been shaped by those outside the Negro community in a way unparalleled in the history of any rising ethnic
group in the nation. This removal of the Negro from the decision-
making role regarding his own destiny has occurred largely over
the past thirty or more years. This removal and isolation together
have meant that not only the Negro community itself but also
the nation as a whole has been bereft of the benefits of much
of the potential which it might have employed to good ends in
many ways.

Significantly, the Negro's heightened sense of isolation and
desperation has grown almost concurrently with the increased
involvement of white leadership in what are largely Negro concerns. This is not to minimize the positive benefits nor to deprecate the manifest sincerity of the interest of others than Negroes

in American race-related problem areas. But the increased leadership of non-Negroes over the past thirty years and more has meant the relative decreasing of the leadership role which Negroes themselves have been able to exercise in areas vitally affecting their own lives and livelihood. This represents a distinctively different pattern from that of all other rising ethnic groups. We have seen in previous chapters some of the crucial statistical evidence reflecting the inherent limitation of such a unique change from the American tradition of ethnic group leadership patterns. More evidence will follow, suggesting and underscoring the need for the leadership of black men to be restored and utilized in new ways in many areas of the nation's life.

By tracing the steps of the relatively recent and singular shift of leadership from Negroes to whites in race-related areas we may come to understand the apparent reasonableness and good faith of the efforts which have led to our present condition. Our understanding of the roots of our present circumstances should further serve the good purpose of creating an atmosphere of mutual appreciation and respect in which the urgently needed new adjustments may best be facilitated for the good of all.

Through the early 1930s Negroes themselves led in what were seen to be largely Negro affairs. This was done through the Negro churches and through the Negro fraternal and other solidarity groups which gave shape to the Negro's own plans and programs for his own destiny.

The white-sponsored organizations for Negro affairs such as the National Urban League and the National Association for the Advancement of Colored People meanwhile played their different and much needed roles. The Urban League, as a social-work organization geared to the orientation of rural Negroes to urban life, in the period of the 1920s and 1930s did not fill the civil rights role which it came to assume increasingly after World War II. The National Association for the Advancement of Colored People was committed to a bi-racial approach to Negro development. White leadership and funds were used in an effort to relate with greater equity the benighted Negro community to the nation's life as a whole. The NAACP's position was characteristically cautious and responsible, as this latter term was perceived through the most sympathetic eyes of those outside of the group which was oppressed. In spite of its prevailing caution, the evident conditions to which the NAACP addressed itself called in the 1920s for moods of militancy which were often expressed by the organization's illustrious Executive Secretary, Walter White. Yet, the spirit of aggressiveness of the NAACP was always circumscribed by the varying pressures and attitudes of the eminent white people who gave to the NAACP most generously of their minds and means. This was inevitable, for in the most crucial ways these people were still outsiders. They could not be either responsive or related to the unremitting inner drive toward freedom and a sense of assertive dignity on the part of the oppressed which alone brings the secure promise of freedom within and so ultimately of freedom without.

The most brilliant spokesman for the Negro's progress into the American mainstream between 1915 and the mid-1930s was the editor of the NAACP's national magazine, *The Crisis*. This was the innately arrogant and aristocratically mannered Dr. William Edward Burghardt DuBois. Dr. DuBois' livelihood and position were continually in the hands of whites whose frequent exasperation with his outspokenness made tenuous the channel by which even this great man could influence his fellow Negro Americans. The Ku Klux Klan moved to new heights of power in a widespread wave of white terror which held sway during the 1920s. DuBois was to react to the widespread savage treatment by whites of their Negro fellow-Americans in the 1920s with the same vitriolic pen which could enable him to speak of the most ordinary Negro as a distinct gentleman when he noted the Negro's meekness and forgiveness before continued white American oppression. Yet he observed that "it takes extraordinary training and opportunity to make the average white man anything but a hog." Such was his contempt of a growing barbarism

—or sustained callousness to it—in the white community as a whole.

During the 1920s Negroes were treated throughout the country in the most savage ways. Lynchings were at their height and were only superficially protested by white people. White America was its most busy ever with the business of laissez-faire superficiality. Its spirit was summed up in the leading character of *Babbitt*. America during the 1920s was admittedly at its insensitive worst. But Negro solidarity grew in the 1920s and expressed itself in an expanding sense of racial pride and in economic, political, and civic self-consciousness. The same period had witnessed both the widening influence of Marcus Garvey's "Back to Africa" movement and the intensified race nationalism of Negroes in their religious and fraternal associations.

The Negroes' trek to the northern cities, and the advent there of waves of black West Indians, uncovered largely the same type of hatred and animosity as other rising ethnic groups previously had met. This served—in the same manner as with other rising ethnic groups—to steel and harden the Negroes into a united front for political, economic, and social change. The bitter and brilliant Dr. DuBois summed up the piercing resentment of the Negro for his long-standing but at last seemingly intolerable abuse at the hands of white Americans. In 1920 the Harvard-trained DuBois condemned in verse what he called "The White World's Vermin and Filth," concluding with the lines:

> I hate them, Oh!
> I hate them well,
> I hate them Christ!
> As I hate hell!
> If I were God
> I'd sound their knell
> This day.

In a sense, the fires for the Negro's aggressive assault on the consciences, the pocketbooks, and the ballot boxes of America had been kindled. As the days of the Great Depression approached the black people of America were poised to make their greatest self-initiated thrust for fuller participation in all aspects of the nation's life. Negroes in those days asked, not for integration, but for an authentically desegregated opportunity to participate with dignity alongside of other Americans with no ethnic distinction. They talked of a not too distant day when legal desegregation would right the awful wrong of the Plessy vs. Ferguson "separate but equal" decision of 1896.

It was in the autumn of 1929 that my brother and I—as six-year-old twins—received an unforgettable lesson which was indicative of the spirit of the times. We were returning home from the local two-room country school in Camp Dennison (near Cincinnati), Ohio. On the way we stopped at a combination country bar and candy store which was assumed to be off-limits to us and was frequented chiefly by poor whites. Our grandmother watched from a distance as we walked along the highway and entered the side door of the bar and candy store to purchase several pieces of penny candy. On reaching home, we received the licking of our lives, as Grandma explained: "If your pennies are good enough to spend, then you're good enough to enter by the front door or not at all!" The spirit in evidence here was characteristic of the pre-depression Negro as he sought desperately to give expression to his own intensely lively sense of dignity and worth.

It was following this period, in the so-called dark years of the depression of the 1930s, that white liberal popular sentiment for the Negro began to grow. White so-called socialists—representing a world-wide phenomenon of the 1930s—showed by many signs their earnest appreciation of their hoped-for black comrades. The movement of the entire nation had been checked by the onslaught of gripping economic stagnation. This included the Negro's anticipated onslaught on the nation's racial patterns. Under such circumstances the socialists looked to the impoverished Negroes of America as potential partners in the coming national and world revolution. This period perhaps marked the Negro's first significant flirtation with the idea of integration as distinct from desegregation. The first public interracial teenage dances that many Negroes ever attended were those sponsored by the young socialists in many northern cities. These were the days which gave the witch-hunters of the 1950s a storehouse of witches to hunt. During the depression era the loudest liberal voices raised on behalf of opportunity and a secure place in American life for Negroes were those of the so-called socialists, the left-wing activists of that day. Almost any young Negro who was then committed to the fulfillment of the American goal of an equitable stake for all in the nation's future had opportunity to come into contact with the socialists. The socialists represented the liberal white people of that period. They offered to the Negro at least a limited sense of reality in an otherwise unreal and seemingly hopeless world.

For the Negro, whose biological and cultural roots were and are more American than any others who comprise America, an international or world revolution did not square with what he had come to dream of for America. With the war clouds gathering before World War II the Negro's enchantment with world revolution, if ever extensive, became depleted. The equalitarian war propaganda of World War II won the Negro's fascination and increased the commitments of white Americans to the improvement of the Negro's lot.

The Turn Toward Integration

Frustrated yet steeled in his efforts toward equality in the 1920s, detoured by the necessities of sheer survival in the 1930s, the Negro of the World War II years had come to a place where he was now open to the propagandized idealism of an interracial solidarity.

It was during the latter 1940s that two developments crucial to an understanding of the Negro's situation today occurred. One

was that the white leadership of Negro affairs came to be generally accepted. The other was that black solidarity came to be
at least shunned, it not scorned, as integration rather than desegregated self-development was acclaimed as the Negro's new
and self-evident goal.

Symbolic of the new interracial brotherhood which was to be
was CORE, the Congress of Racial Equality, which came into
existence in the early 1940s. Like the NAACP and the National
Urban League, CORE was largely white-led and largely white-
financed. The galaxy of CORE's white sponsors had the supple-
mentary color of several eminent Negro leaders of national stature. In reality CORE was, during the first decade and more of
its existence, the race-relations arm of the pacifist Fellowship of
Reconciliation. CORE has always had a particular appeal to
youth. At the end of World War II, CORE offered, as an antidote to the disillusionment of the violence of the war, an outlet
for the expression of an idealism aimed at the vindication in part
of the war's stated domestic goals.

CORE's first significant move toward national prominence
came with its sponsorship of its first Freedom Ride, then called
the Journey of Reconciliation, in 1947. The tour extended
through five states of the upper South testing and implementing
the then recent Irene Morgan Decision outlawing segregation in
public interstate travel. CORE's membership was largely white,
and its program of nonviolent direct action became a model for
increased and effective efforts at the lowering of barriers to Negroes in all forms of public accommodation, in housing, and in
some forms of employment. CORE's greatest contribution in a
growing atmosphere of interraciality undoubtedly was its promotion of a growing sense of adventure, coupled with apparent success with regard to efforts in the field of civil rights.

This spirit of adventure caught hold in the Montgomery, Ala-
bama, bus boycotts, in the southern student lunch-counter desegregation efforts, and in the massive drives in the 1960s for the
creation and implementation of opportunities for Negroes in

northern and southern voter registration, housing, employment, and educational desegregation.

The outcome of the 1954 Supreme Court Brown *vs.* Board of Education school desegregation case added to the idealism and enthusiasm of the integration-minded endeavors of the times. Indeed the decision gave legal sanction to the growing conviction that integration must be a national ideal. In line with this same spirit, churches and civic groups worked in conscious and unconscious ways to check and thwart the development of Negro solidarity. White church denominations made bold their plans to build no more churches in Negro areas, as only interraciality was seen to be consistent with the churches' missionary enterprise. Negroes in large numbers left Negro churches, as the prestige of specifically Negro institutions drastically declined. Negro business endeavors tended to be discouraged, as only integrated institutions were to be encouraged in the days ahead. Debate came to center around the future role of Negro colleges, since it seemed abundantly clear that the long-expected day of equity and opportunity for the Negro had come at last.

Meanwhile, there were growing signs that all was not well, that things were not wholly what they had seemed to be. In the early 1960s there were symptoms of increasing conflict and tension in urban centers of the North, as well as no permanent peace in the technically desegregated areas of the South. This seemed strange in view of the nation's heightened commitment to interraciality and to civil rights.

A Checking of the Score

A concern for the growing dissatisfaction in the face of seeming racial progress led in several directions. It led to a psychological analysis and to a critical checking of the score to find out just what type of "progress" it was that had been steadily hailed for several decades.

The psychological analysis was a rather simple one. Its major estimate was that the opening of new doors to opportunity for Negro Americans was responsible for whetting the appetites for further opportunity at a faster rate than it was possible to satisfy them. Hence, both frustration and a sense of anger at the more lively realization of past denials of opportunity. This analysis suggests that the riots have stemmed largely from too great hope's having been given the Negro by those in America who have sought to forward the cause of civil rights.

The conclusion here overlooks the most significant catalyst for world change, the United Nations. Its forum holds up to the world's view the record of redemption of the pledges of every nation of the world for freedom and equity in the relationships of its people. It may be at least as reasonable, therefore, to assume that had there been no great commitment to civil rights leadership and initiative on the part of white Americans, there might have been an even greater and more profitable testing for the nation. Negroes themselves, for one thing, would have had to carry the banners for their own growing place in the nation's life, as each other rising ethnic group has had to do. Doubtless the pressures of world opinion would have quickened the efforts of Negroes toward this end, and doubtless also the nation would have had either to respond in positive and substantial ways or to turn its back more clearly upon its commitment to democratic goals. In either case, the record of precisely where the nation stands would be more easy to read than it is now, and the Negro would undoubtedly have brought about for himself the greater respect of others through the empowering processes of self-directed initiative and self-development.

The critical checking of the score to discover the precise nature of the reputed gains which had been made for Negroes revealed startling results which contradicted the ready perceptions of many who had been intimately involved in the battle for civil rights.

As to economic progress, we have noted earlier that there has been no clear statistical trend toward a closing of the economic gap between whites and non-whites over a period of nearly twenty years. Dollar-wise, Negroes have retreated in relation to white in-come; percentage-wise the trend remains uncertain. Thus the shouts of progress have no clear base in fact. As white leadership in Negro economic-opportunity creation has grown, the situation with regard to the Negro's relative stake in a growing economy has not improved.

Many Negroes and white people point with satisfaction and pride at job opportunities being opened to Negroes. Indeed, new jobs are being opened every day. In some categories where suffi-cient workers could not be found, Negroes have been given pri-ority of opportunity. Further, many businesses, along with gov-ernment and civic agencies who are concerned with the relative dollar-wise worsening of the lot of the masses of Negroes in our central cities, have made heroic efforts at the creation of new jobs and the opening of new opportunities for Negroes. The U.S. De-partment of Commerce, the U.S. Labor Department, and the fed-eral Office of Economic Opportunity have combined their efforts with those of other federal, state, local, and private agencies in opening new avenues to Negro employment. In spite of these substantial efforts in good faith, however, the plight of Negroes has not been effectively improved.

The crucial point is that it is not the amount of the input of effort which makes for the proper results. Only the right kind of input can bring about, in any circumstances, the desired results. What is needed for the Negro's condition to be improved—and so for the nation's economic life and civil security to be preserved—is the kind of creative insight and intensity of commitment which can only come from the leadership of those who are immediately oppressed. Thus it has always been, where any substantial sem-blance of success has been achieved by rising ethnic groups. This does not exclude the need for the generous resources, involve-ment and commitment of others. But the proof of the pudding has been in the eating with regard to the obtaining of the desired re-sults. The moving forward of Negro opportunity in relation to growing opportunities and needs in our economy is a bit like com-

paring the progress of a dog-sled to that of a speeding train. Dog
sleds can do well; they can make "progress." But when the circumstances of the times move much faster than our means of
progress, then it becomes increasingly doubtful as to whether the
terms "progress" or "gains" may legitimately apply.

Table number I indicates the "Measures of Progress in Defense
Jobs and in General Business" by Negro employees and by all
employees for the years 1962 or 1963 and 1964.

TABLE I [1]

MEASURES OF PROGRESS

IN DEFENSE JOBS

Only a few of the statistical pictures of the progress of Negroes toward
new and better jobs are reliable. The President's Committee on Equal
Employment Opportunity is a prime source. It gets reports from prime
contractors and first-level subcontractors who hold government contracts
for $50,000 or more and employ 50 or more workers. Reports from
3,471 plants show this progress from 1962 to 1964:

All employees

	1962	1964	Percent increase
Total	2,049,064	2,111,864	3.1
White-collar	775,033	832,774	7.5
Blue-collar	1,274,031	1,279,090	0.4

Negro employees

Total	136,613	146,880	7.5
White-collar	12,079	15,782	30.7
Blue-collar	124,534	131,098	5.3

IN GENERAL BUSINESS

Plans for Progress is another program run by the same committee. It's a
voluntary program in which 308 companies with 8.6 million employees
have promised to go beyond legal requirements in giving employment
opportunities to non-whites. This is the picture of progress from 1963 to
1964 shown in reports from 100 of these companies with about 4 million
employees:

All employees

	1963	1964	Percent increase
Total	3,969,748	4,090,361	3.0
White-collar	1,887,437	1,905,144	0.9
Blue-collar	2,082,311	2,185,217	4.9

Non-white employees

	1963	1964	Percent increase
Total	232,692	266,317	14.5
White-collar	40,553	47,134	16.2
Blue-collar	192,139	219,183	14.1

When this data is looked at in the light of projected employment needs in 1975, the critical nature of the relationship between means and ends in Negro employment opportunity should become more evident. Table Number II reveals "Employment by Major Occupation Group, 1964, and Projected Requirements, 1975."

TABLE II [2]

Employment by major occupation group, 1964, and projected requirements, 1975

Major occupation group	1964		1975		Percent change 1964-75
	Number (in millions)	Per-cent	Number (in millions)	Per-cent	
Total employment ...	70.4	100.0	88.7	100.0	26%
White-collar workers	31.1	44.2	42.8	48.3	38
Professional, technical, and kindred workers ...	8.6	12.2	13.2	14.9	54
Managers, officials, and proprietors, except farm	7.5	10.6	9.2	10.4	23
Clerical and kindred workers	10.7	15.2	14.6	16.5	37
Sales workers	4.5	6.3	5.8	6.5	30
Blue-collar workers	25.5	36.3	29.9	33.7	17
Craftsmen, foremen, and kindred workers	9.0	12.8	11.4	12.8	27

Operatives and kindred workers	12.9	18.4	14.8	16.7	15
Laborers, except farm and mine	3.6	5.2	3.7	4.2	*
Service workers	9.3	13.2	12.5	14.1	35
Farmers and farm managers, laborers, and foremen	4.4	6.3	3.5	3.9	−21

* Less than 3%

The February 1966 Report of the National Commission on Technology, Automation, and Economic Progress comments as follows in reference to the needs projected to 1975:

These changes in occupational requirements have significant implications for certain groups in the labor force. If nonwhites continue to hold the same proportion of jobs in each occupation as in 1964, the non-white unemployment rate in 1975 will be more than five times that for the labor force as a whole. In 1964, the unemployment rate of nonwhites was 9.8 percent, about twice that for whites. *If trends in upgrading the jobs of nonwhites continue at the same rate as in recent years,* the non-white unemployment rate in 1975 would still be about 2½ times that for the labor force as a whole. Thus nonwhites must gain access to the rapidly growing higher skilled and white-collar occupations at a faster rate than in the past 3 years if the unemployment rate is to be brought down to the common level.[3]

The nation's internal peace, its external commitments to the enlargement of freedom, and its own will to bring fulfillment to its people cannot accommodate the past and present pattern of endeavors in the interests of equitable employment relationships. However altruistic they may be or have been, their transparent inadequacy must come to command replacement by new and effective mechanisms for employment pattern adjustment. It is clear also that efforts at lower echelon job training for Negroes should not be given the priority which they have enjoyed. Negroes need immediate employment *at all levels,* and especially at the higher levels, using talents and skills already developed and available. New mechanisms and the coordination of old mechanisms in vastly new frameworks, with the kind of commitment which dictates the utilization of black men's leadership, are called for *at the very least.* The nation cannot afford to have its major source of civil malaise incessantly subjected to pilot projects, or used as the pawn in a political chess game, when massive efforts calling for the maximum of commitment and the clearest insights are needed in the most urgent way.

As white leadership in American race-related concerns has grown, we have not only failed to achieve desired economic progress, in spite of the greatest good faith and sincerity. In addition, we have not overcome the accelerated growth of other significant problem areas. A summary of the record for the period in which white leadership in race-related matters has come to be well-nigh complete, might be as follows:

1. School segregation in the North has increased.
2. Residential segregation has increased.
3. The dollar-income gap between whites and Negroes has increased.
4. The division between the Negro poor and the leadership natively related to them has increased.
5. Negro self-hate, as estimated by the growing crimes of violence and social patterns of self-destruction (including riots), has increased.
6. The compromise of Negro professionals, under so-called integrated arrangements where white men still hold the reins of power, has grown apace.
7. The social and economic costs to the nation of mounting relief roles have increased.
8. The national debility from its failure to utilize its fullest resources and insights in the resolution of its many unsolved problems may be assumed to have increased.

9. The failure to make commitments *of the depth and order of priority clearly called for* has meant that the imminent danger of social conflagration and civil disaster has tremendously increased.

In addition to the above items, in a record revealing the tragic but unintended inadequacy of present instruments for progress in race-related areas, under white leadership in Negro affairs a further unfortunate development occurred.

10. A change was made in the goal for Negro Americans which differed radically from the goal of all other rising ethnic groups. Under white leadership in Negro efforts at development, the universal goal of desegregation was changed to that of integration.

It may be seen that the foisting of this latter goal upon the Negro has been like the placing of an albatross upon the necks of Negroes. It has become the primary source of needless and growing conflict in the cities and the suburbs of the nation. No other rising ethnic group in America has asked for more than desegregation. This is all that Negroes undoubtedly, under sustained Negro leadership, would have sought. Desegregation of any authenticity would have involved in the South greater pupil interchange, as students would attend schools with either programs *or* geographical proximity best suited to their needs. The same principles would prevail in the North. No artificial barriers would separate and divide. Equal opportunity and equal access to enabling relationships could have been and still can be developed within the frameworks of genuine desegregation alone.

Negroes should long ago have perceived that enforced "integration" as a goal is a compromise of black Americans on its face. Negroes do not need the presence of white people either to give them worth or to learn. No artificial barriers as now exist, however, should be allowed to continue. Desegregation includes substantial integration, but only as an incidental ingredient and not as a sought-for goal. This is all that America needs to promise. This is neither more nor less than what every other rising ethnic group in America has asked for. From a position of secure desegregation, Negroes may then develop the power to move ahead and to add their potential to other power-producing levers for the further enrichment of the life of the nation as a whole.

The Potential Function of Black Leadership

Black leadership should have been given, over the past thirty and more years, in largely Negro affairs. Such leadership must be given in the future. The deviation from the customary course of indigenous leadership for freedom struggles and for efforts at self-development is as understandable as it has proven to be unprofitable. The emphasis upon relationships, it must be repeated, is in the crucial role of leadership alone. No problem in American life touches only one segment of the nation's life. Every American must be involved in more effective, power-producing mechanisms. It is chiefly the relationships within the framework of the already existing involvement which are brought into question here.

Negro leadership in various aspects of American life may be seen to be advantageous and necessary for the nation's fulfillment in several specific ways. We have suggested thus far that Negro leadership alone may bring about the kind of self-development which will afford the hope of authentic progress in race-related problem areas. Progress, in the strictest sense of the word, has not been made. We have moved forward but American life as a whole has moved at a faster rate than the rate of Negro gains. This is not progress. It is at the very least stagnation. It represents a clear frustration of the American goal to secure the blessings of the American way of life to all of the nation's citizens. The blame belongs to no particular group; we are all indicted. We have all been involved, in varying ways, in the historical processes both profitable and unprofitable which have brought us where we are. It devolves upon all of us as a nation to speedily shift our gears and to assume the new leadership and enabling or power-producing roles which will make for America's fulfillment by bringing about growth into self-directed self-sufficiency on the part of Negro Americans. Competent black men and women should hold their share of executive positions in civic, religious, and business organizations, where they can make use of their saving insights. Short of this, we will have continued malfunctions, increased waste and growing unrest in the institutions associated with our urban life.

Again, through the use of black leadership in race-related problem areas we may reshape present goals for Negro Americans so as to be far more consonant with broad goals for all Americans. Numerous Negro leadership groups have complained increasingly over the past several years that programs designed specifically for Negroes are really adequate for nobody. For Negroes are more than members of a benighted racial group. They are part and parcel of America. The growing uncouthness of many young Americans and the lazy habits of thought which are inevitably associated with low incentives reflect problems that are broadly pervasive in America. All Americans over twenty-one years of age may help in the making of decisions which are critical for the nation's life; and we do not educate for the kind of responsible outlooks which can assure the maintenance and extension of our democratic way of life. The New York City subway strike of 1966 is a clear example of the growing tendency to settle disputes or problems in American life with more force than rationality. Labor alone is not guilty; nor is it the most guilty, as many might tend to believe. The use of force to arbitrate disputes is a growing characteristic throughout American life. Education in liberating studies and in creative avocations should be coupled with every endeavor to educate Americans for a fuller life. Life, as well as livelihood, must be prepared for in America.

We must begin a reassessment of every problem area adversely affecting Negro Americans to discover how the problems may be approached in saving ways for all Americans. The unused insights of black scholars and leaders and of all participants in what is in some ways the richly rewarding life of black Americans must be used for this purpose. Unless plans for Negroes are good for America as a whole, they are not fundamentally good for Negro Americans.

Negro leadership has been, without question, the most sensitive to the weaknesses in American life. This leadership needs to be used at high levels in both business and government and in all aspects of our institutional life, if fulfillment in these several areas is to be our goal. The blind spots which white Americans have developed to adjust to our cultural customs, with their built-in racist limitations, can be overcome with the swiftness that they need to be, by the equitable and immediate use of Negro leadership potential which is now available. The myth that Negroes need training, which is only partly true, as all myths are, allows those responsible in and for American government, business, and other institutions to overlook the ready resources for their own good and gain available immediately in the Negro community. The equitable immediate employment of these underemployed resources would represent in itself the fulfillment of the American goal of efficiency in productiveness issuing in the maximum of good returns.

The use of black leadership, finally, would involve the catalyzing of a new and much needed process of equitable interchange in American life. Negroes and whites in America need to be engaged in dialogue which is creative by virtue of its authentic give and take. For simple survival, Negroes have been the most sensitive observers of American life. Their lives as well as their livelihood have depended upon such sensitivity to an extent far different from the experience of all other ethnic groups. It is time for America to cash in on an unexpected resource which it has built without its own knowing. Black leadership thus may begin to lead America at this crucial hour toward a clearer vision and more realistic fulfillment of goals basic to the nation's coming into its own.

IX

A Religious Opportunity

There are no institutions which have more to gain from the current focus on Black Power than the churches of America, both black and white. The churches, in both conscious and unconscious ways, have contributed toward the resurgence of racial self-awareness and the assertion of dignity and self-respect which Black Power represents. In return, the churches may receive their greatest boost and challenge for their own cleansing, regeneration and fulfillment.

Fulfillment

Black Power, in its simplest terms, speaks to the nature of humanity. The greatest problem before the churches, and before every institution in our world, is some form of the human problem. What is the human goal? Toward what end should every aspect of human life be directed? The answer given by the current impetus toward Black Power is the one word *fulfillment*.

The black people of America want to fulfill their potential, for their own good and for the larger enrichment of the common store of all Americans. To become what one must be demands the presence, the building up, of power. Centuries ago Aristotle made what has since become the most classic expression of human destiny. He declared that what a thing will be, that it is, whether it be a horse or a man. The unstated ingredient which he assumed was the presence of power. All men need the power to *become*. Indeed, the Greek words for power (*bia*) and life (*bios*) reflect the essential interrelationship of power and life. Power is basic to life. Without power, life cannot become what it must be.

In order to respond effectively to the human problem, institutions concerned with ultimate social ends must be power-producing enterprises. They must be or become enablers, facilitating human growth into self-direction toward its appointed flower and fulfillment. Conversely, any agency which promotes dependency or which limits self-directed progress toward maturity and self-sufficiency complicates the human problem. It warps the human condition and subverts the divine purpose of human growth.

In religious terms, a God of power, of majesty and of might, who has made man to be in His own image and likeness, must will that His creation reflect in the immediacies of life His power, His majesty and His might. Black Power raises, for the healing of humanity and for the renewal of a commitment to the creative religious purpose of growth, the far too long overlooked need for power, if life is to become what in the mind of its Creator it is destined to be.

So often in religious life in America we have tended to settle for less than ultimate goals. We have courted the illusory separate but equal despoiler of human growth. We have sought to do our level and most conscientious best within the frameworks of class and pseudo-caste which forbade the fulfillment of God's design for His creation. We have fed men lavishly, where a sense of the divine purpose of human growth should have prompted our teaching of men to feed themselves *and* our affording them the sustained and equitable opportunity for self-provision. Power is essential to life. Men may kill and destroy as wantonly by smothering, by too much uncritically-thought-out kindness, as by neglect. The Black Power issue here recalls the churches—and every institution concerned with the human condition—to the employment of critical judgment in every intention to facilitate human growth. We must worship God—and serve our fellow man—with our minds as well as with our hearts. The head and heart must be reunited in the religious enterprise. To feel kindly disposed may be lethal, if one's kindliness is not wedded to in- formed and tempered judgment.

The churches, then, must constantly keep before them the purpose of human growth. The programs and policies of the churches must be planned and re-examined continually from this perspective. Is human potential being thwarted in its effort to become what it must be? From such a perspective or frame of reference as this, a far more creative attitude would need to be developed in many areas of the life of our religious institutions. We could no longer effectively restrict the opportunities for service by clergy whose minds and hearts are formed for great- ness and extensive service but whose skins are darker than what a racist-ridden secular culture might desire. For what ends are we to settle? Which gods, to put it more clearly, are we to wor- ship? Not only would such a race-related question be asked. We would also need to raise new questions concerning the utilization of retired persons, the employment of female skills, the right incentives for Christian stewardship, and the specifics of Chris- tian service in the world. The power issue thus holds the key for the opening of many doors.

Every parish clergyman might measure the fruitfulness of his tasks by their relationship to the furtherance of power. Have I created dependency? Or have I facilitated self-directed growth? This is the root question as it relates to the human condition with our families, with friends and in every personal and cor- porate relationship in life. It is the enduring issue in our civic life in reference to the schools. It bears upon the kind of charity with which we face the condition of the aged. Every life yearns, or should yearn, for growth and for fulfillment. It should always be facilitated toward that very end.

It is crucial to understand the role of pain in the pattern of growth. "No pain, no progress" is a dictum of universal applicability. At the center of life, so the Christian contends, is a cross. It is "the emblem of suffering and shame." It may be painful to us to allow another to suffer in order for growth to be facilitated. But the mothers of infants, the teachers of adolescents and those associated with the medical arts all know just how essential pain is to human growth. We must often forego apparent little kindnesses to do the larger and far kinder thing. We must even more often forego—aggressively, graciously and single-mindedly—the caprice of the unkind customs of the communities and of households of which we are a part, "lest we make the word of God to no effect through our traditions."

Life yearns for fulfillment. The churches of America—as they are attentive and attuned to the need for power on the part of all—must turn, in ways which are marks of religious regeneration, toward the central and most enduring task of human life. They may work, as God would will, for the empowerment of life to become what He would have it be.

Focus

The Black Power concept is startling. It brings into focus an apparent incongruity in associating power with those whom our culture conditions us to think of as powerless. Could there be anything more ludicrous than a powerful half-grown child? It is like speaking of vigorous laziness or discontented contentedness. It is hard for those conditioned by our American racist-ridden culture, to accept blackness and power in one breath. Even many Negroes, who often out-hate their white fellow-Americans when it comes to loathing blackness, think of it as unseemly to compound the term Black Power.

Yet our religious life should enable us to bring into new and more creative focus things which otherwise we might not see and understand. Our religious life should enable us to see all reality in the light of Ultimate Reality. In this sense, those who practice the presence of God and would "see God face to face" must inevitably grow in the capacity of seeing the face of God not beyond, but in and through, the face of every man. Nonetheless the most common American experience is for racial bigotry to increase as apparent religiosity increases. Witness the relation of whites in the Bible Belt to blacks of the almost identical area called the Black Belt. Fundamentalism and intolerance are more than incidentally related. There is no evidence of increased inter-marriage—which historically is the most natural of all forms of human interchange—among "the Spirit-filled." Nor is there a greater evident commitment to human fulfillment and racial inter-change among monastic or conventual communities. There is an evident inherent basic flaw in any religious experience which can-not unloose and move beyond a deadly cultural bind or limitation.

The seeming incongruity of blackness and power, in the face of the need for all men to appropriate power for human growth, reminds us of the vital need for a new focus to be brought to bear on human life. A possible clue to a resolution of our predicament lies in the glorification aspect of the Black Power emphasis. Blackness—which includes by definition all shades and complex-ions of non-whiteness—has been degraded in our culture. The glorification of blackness implicit in the term Black Power is a conscious or unconscious effort to stake a claim for the worth of those in our nation who are termed non-white. Essentially it is a clarification. The root meaning of the term "glorify" is to clarify, to make clear and plain and straight.

All of life must be clarified in this sense. It must be given and seen in that dimension which sets it forth in terms of glory—now and forever. To see life as it truly is means to see it as God sees it, in its eternal dimension, in the glory appropriate to its involvement with and in the life of God. Is not another way of looking at the purpose of fulfillment to see as the end of all life its transfiguration, its glorification, its clarification for what it is in the mind and vision and will of the agency of its creation?

Our worship, for example, should be directed to this purpose. It should reflect life in its most clear and untarnished sense. The life of the ancient church, the church in its earlier centuries, tended to reflect this aspect of religious purpose far more than does the worship of the church today. The spirit of the ancient church in this regard must be recaptured. We may see this aspect of clarification or glory in several of the main features of the worship of the early church.

The worship of the early Christian church was familial in character. Its setting reflected this quality of its life. The worshipping congregation gathered around a family table. At the head of the table was the father of the family, who sat in the seat of Christ. Here he presided over what many other members of the family of God did in corporate worship. From his seat at the head of the table, that is, behind it and facing the family, the president or priest or bishop also taught the lessons of the faith to those of the household of faith. Worship took place in the atmosphere of an intimate family gathering. The church tended to sense a oneness in Christ, similar in spirit to the historical family oneness of the Jews, but transcendng and enfolding the limits of physical lineage. It was St. Augustine who gave the classic expression to the early church's sense of being a family, and so of fashioning or welding all of human life into the oneness which the church realized in Christ. Writing of the undesirability of marriage between blood or close relatives, St. Augustine gave utterance to the early church's sense of relationship, either actual or potential, with all of human life. The church sensed a need, in the most deeply human terms, to make of the human race one blood-related family within the household of faith. St. Augustine explained:

The first of all marriages was that between the man made out of dust and his mate who had issued from his side. After that, the continuance and increase of the human race demanded births from the union of males and females, even though there were no other human beings except those born of the first two persons. That is why men took their sisters for wives.

But, of course, just as this is the best thing to do when natural necessity compels it, it becomes all the more wicked when moral obligation condemns it. This can be proved as follows. The human law is love and this law is best respected when men, who both desire and ought to live in harmony, so bind themselves by the bonds of social relationships that no one man monopolizes more than one relationship, and many different relationships are distributed as widely as possible, so that a common social life of the greatest number may best be fostered.[1]

St. Augustine takes his position a step further, indicating that the more diverse the population the more the faithful should chose in marriage those most distant from them in race, clan, province, culture or nation. In this way those of the church might express the oneness of the human family in Christ.

The religious institutions of America may make a saving reassessment—with the focus here afforded by the issue of Black Power—of the interrelated nature of human life. The assumption of the kind of oneness held by those in the early church is manifestly lacking in the church today. Our focus is not their focus. Yet the familial nature of the Christian life is consistent with their conception of the nature and destiny of human life.

The worship of the ancient church was marked by a hierarchical framework of relationships. There were different or specialized roles to perform. But the filling of these roles was open to all. Thus the Roman Pontiff at the time of the Peace of Constantine was a man of black African descent. Pope Melchiades led the Church at Rome through its last days of illegality into the period of its final legal recognition. Although slavery was accepted, it bore scarcely any more connotations of inferiority within the church, or outside of it, than did foreign citizenship. The ranks of the church were open to all and the inherent dynamics of the church tended to empty slavery of its low status. The focus of the church was upon life seen as it should be—and is eternally—and according to which pattern it must therefore be lived in the here and now.

The worship of the early church was marked by a depth of individual and corporate participation by many and by all which is lacking in the church today. The chief pastor presided over what others did singly and collectively. He was a facilitater, an enabler, rather than a star performer. All who desire the growth of others into their due fulfillment should be enablers. They should help others to grow in the self-directing power to become what they should be. All in the early church participated in the ministry to the sick and others. Today we must doubtless learn in the church that even the sick can minister, bringing healing to themselves as they engage in therapeutic acts on behalf of others. The aged too, or perhaps especially, have more time and more maturity for tasks in the church and outside of it calling for the skills and other gifts of the unhurried and the wise. The Black Power emphasis upon the maximum use of all human potential for the greater good of all suggests for the churches perhaps untapped human resources which are ripe for the church's harvesting.

The worship of the ancient church brought a further sense of clarity or focus upon the nature of the church's life through its use of sacred writings. The lessons from the Old and the New Testaments were read as family history. The Epistles were intimate letters of the family, alive with the feelings of those bound by close-knit ties. The Old Testament readings were lessons in family lore, a reminder of the family heritage of those who were spiritually, and so essentially, the sons of Abraham. The Scriptures reflected in this setting a life or inheritance into which one had already entered, rather than a system of beliefs to which one must give assent. The Scripture readings were experiences in being. Knowledge of Christ was not so much fact-knowledge as it was the knowledge of relationship, as in the knowing of one's wife or husband. It was life of one in another, in the sense in which St. Paul speaks of life "in Christ."

Finally, the worship of the early church brought a new sense of focus or of clarification in that its essential act of thanksgiving, or of Eucharist as it was called, involved the transfiguration or the lifting of life onto a plane where it befitted the purpose of God. Utilizing the earthy symbols of bread, water and wine, every aspect of life was symbolically reunited with its Originator, Sustainer and End. Life was glorified. Indeed, it always was and is so on the level of the eternal, which was and is the true; and so the church simply had to make Eucharist or to give thanks for the clarification or for the glory of life which is forever a constant in the mind, experience and sight of God. What *will be* on an eternal plane *is now* for those who, with thankfulness for God's doings, enter into the realities which are as yet to be revealed. The ancients may be said to have sensed that "It does not yet appear what we shall be, but when Christ who is our life shall appear, we shall appear with him in glory, for we shall see him as he is." [2] The mind of the early Church was expressed when Tertullian wrote, *"Christianus alter Christus,"* the Christian is another Christ. Every Christian was a revelation of Christ. Can Christians denigrate or restrict or deface the life of Christ in their black brothers and still be called by the name of Christ?

By clear implication, the Black Power concept may both chasten and challenge the churches of America to at least focus upon the realities which they are called both to see and be. American religion needs to be regenerated. Black Power, as a concept emphasizing the need to bring a different focus to bear upon life itself and its possibilities, may open a pathway toward the renewal of American religious life. [3]

Self-Concept

No programs of renewal by themselves will lead to any re-creative trends in American religion. The churches of America must have a new self-concept and a firm determination to fulfill it. A self-concept is developed chiefly by one's secure alignment with power. This is true of children as their personalities are structured through the power dynamics of the home. This is true of young adults as they are Americanized and incorporate something of the force of the nation's life into their lives. This is the way that adults find identification in their communities and in every circle of relationships. They identify with power or create new blocs of power. It is through the tensions and coalescence of power that families are formed and shaped. The power of wives and husbands in creative tension and coalescence allows for adult growth and produces the atmosphere which determines the unique character of families and ultimately to a great degree the character of the nation itself.

The clergy and the churches of America are no exception to this rule. They either identify with existing power or they form new associations of power. Power is essential to institutional and professional being and performance. The fully evident need for a new type of power base by the black people of America has led logically to a reaching after the collective power of those whom racism in America have effectively disinherited. In this endeavor the churches have begun to play a unique and vital part. Potentially all the churches of America have much to gain from the current focus on Black Power.

Numbers of Negro clergy have seen in Black Power the means of restoring to themselves, as well as to the Negro churches, a new sense of integrity and self-respect. Thus the National Committee of Negro Churchmen has taken a leadership role across the nation both in promoting the positive aspects of Black Power and in encouraging its extensive development in every black community in the land. In this endeavor they have themselves been encouraged by growing numbers of white churchmen. Some of these have shared continually in thoughtful analyses of the social role of the churches in American life. Others are from among those who have found in the power issue an unexpected source of potential vitality and new meaning, perhaps as never before in their religious life. There has been a mounting realization that the self-concept not only of the Negro churchmen of America but also of the churches as a whole has been wanting. Indeed, what many see as the current crisis in American religion reflects the need for a new sense of wholeness, integrity, and common purpose on the part of all the churches of America.[4]

We have noted how the churches can benefit pastorally from the implications of Black Power which re-emphasize growth-producing mechanisms and goals. The churches have at least as much to gain in their prophetic role. It is always good to have a sense of purpose in one's life. But if one senses its affinity with cosmic purpose, it puts a spring in one's step and gives a tone to one's spirit which spells vibrancy and a quiet sense of confidence and command. Such has been the spirit of countless churchmen who through the recent raising of the issue of power have a new sense of purpose. One white clergyman told that, although he had not admitted it, he had yearned to leave the ministry until he experienced a sense of awakening with the raising of issues afforded by Black Power. He explained that the only way he could accomplish things in his ministry was by aligning himself with one form of power or another among the businessmen or among the matrons who had long assumed and exercised a kind of proprietary trust over every aspect of the parish life. These lords and ladies of the enterprise allowed him to preach whatever he wanted, within limits, and especially so long as no implementation of prophetic notions was expected. He had been well provided for, and no great demands were made upon him. But he saw himself increasingly as being under house arrest, as the kept person in a kind of illicit enterprise where religion was used, unconsciously perhaps but no less effectively, for something considerably less than the purposes of God.

The clergyman went on to explain that issues raised by the focus on Black Power had the effect of turning him on and of providing a new sense of both his being and his vocation. He saw in the Black Power idea, and in those persons associated with it, a new source of his own personal strength and a new avenue to significant relationships. He felt that he could now speak to his people with a new sense of integrity about race relations, as Black Power focused interest not upon what is due the Negro but upon what the black people of America are seeking to add in terms of the enrichment of American life. Who in his parish could object to the lesser taxes from a reduction of the high tariff now paid for relief? Who could object to the development on the part of any benighted segment of the community of the kind of impressive self-respect which commands the admiration and confidence of others? Who could object to the determination on the part of those representing hitherto overlooked resources to add their insights and services to the broad confrontation of issues in our local, national and international life? He felt, and sensed that his congregation would feel the same, that God knows that at this juncture in our corporate life we need the help of all. Black Power was, in his mind, a gift like grace to American life. In his teaching, preaching, and pastoral services, he saw for himself and his congregation new possibilities for a new and more dynamic self-awareness.

Essential to the operation of any institution is the lively and common recognition of its own nature and purpose. The literature of Christian witness is replete with how-to-do and what-has-been done prescriptions. But most often overlooked is the recognition that only from the point of self-awareness—such as that to which Black Power addresses itself for American Negroes—can authentic self-directed and growth-producing activities be performed. The church in America has lacked self-awareness. It has failed to see itself in the same lively terms as did the ancient church. It was seen then as a living organism, extending the life of God in the world. Seen as an organism, it is clear that conscious growth toward the fulfillment of the purposes inherent in its life need to be fostered. It can be recognized that only by its own proper nurture can its functions outside its life be performed. Unless the church has a genuine inner life, it cannot have an authentic outer life. Those who are self-aware know that their basic goal is not to *go* somewhere but simply to *be* what they potentially are, in and through each present circumstance in life.

The clergyman who moved toward a new sense of self-awareness finally indicated that he felt that there were no more exciting prospects before him than in helping his people to ascertain new forms of outreach in the Negro community.

Service

Just how can white young people and adults assist in projects relating to the Negro community in ways consistent with the impetus toward Black Power?

For those in the churches, the most immediate recognition must be that any project is more an expression of one's being than it is of one's outreach. As it is true of the churches, so it is true of America as a whole: Bringing the kind of fulfillment to all of America to which Black Power addresses itself must be seen as a need inherent in the nation's being and that of its every citizen. The greatest area of need is in the conversion of every American to the idea of moving America toward its destiny by developing and utilizing the full potential of all. In this endeavor we must begin where we are. White Americans inevitably will find in their present primary associations and relationships in the white community plenty of opportunity for conversion and enlistment. The best forms of change are always those which begin among our personal or primary relationships in prompt and unobtrusive ways.

In the American culture it is well-nigh impossible for any of us to escape racist assumptions and involvements. Simply witness the way we marry, which indicates clearly that in basic human relationships involving the deepest mutuality and interchange white Americans do not choose to include non-whites, those whom we consider "something else." The same cannot be proved to be equally true of Negroes. It is not they who make the laws or define the taboos and customs of the land. A group-dynamics laboratory experience demonstrated the nature of the problem which we face. A member of the group, which comprised about eight Negroes and four white people, remarked that she had no racial prejudice and was very fond of Negroes. A training group laboratory standard is a thoroughgoing honesty, and in this spirit a white group trainer replied: "That's interesting. I hate Negroes. . . ." After a brief pause, he continued explaining: "My cultural upbringing makes me that way. But I do my best to control and overcome it." The woman who spoke of having no racial prejudice quickly got the message. American life infects us all with its limitations. We must be honest with ourselves, and be mindful of the subtle ways in which our upbringing—in the light of the historical experience of our nation—will inevitably tend to make us other than what our ideals decree. Before we can engage in activities fruitfully with others, we must be mindful at least of the need to be self-aware in this regard. In this way, we can generate or further stimulate our own growth, and by our openness to our own limitations we can minimize the possibility of undue offense to others.

Close to home still, we can serve the needs of the Negro community by deliberately creating opportunities for black people to work in and relate to our communities in ways perhaps hitherto untried. As school officials, as clergymen, as professionals in other capacities, we may ask whether such opportunities as these have been opened equitably to Negroes in the towns or cities where we live. Correcting imbalances in an imbalanced culture must always be done in arbitrary and calculated ways until the cultural pattern itself is changed. Then again, we may ask some further questions. Do Negroes belong to my country club or business or other group? And if not, why not? In how many ways am I the beneficiary of opportunities arbitrarily denied to others? Another way of putting this last question is: How do growth possibilities open to me limit unfairly the growth possibilities of others? Do I unconsciously lessen the dignity or worth of any human life?

A pressing need, emphasized throughout this entire discussion of Black Power and urban unrest, is for the creation of many forms of dialogue designed to facilitate continuing and accelerating changes in every community. We can serve the needs in the Negro community by devising local forums for white people, and encouraging Negroes and mixed groups to do the same, for discussions concerning the myriad implications of the principles of growth and fulfillment. We can do this in reference to our business life and in regard to our social, religious and civic life. In this way, we may build mechanisms for broader and continuing changes throughout the life of our communities. Here it may be underscored once more that our confrontation with the issue of Black Power may open up for us approaches long needed, and doubtless more greatly needed for the future, to many problems which might otherwise have been more difficult to treat.

In every community and institution in America, group laboratory dynamics could profitably be taught. Those who teach always grow through every teaching experience. The force of all that is said in these pages is that here—in the Black Power issue—may be an unexpected once-in-a-lifetime kind of opportunity for America, and all of its institutions, to face with the greatest ease and effectiveness the growing needs and challenges presented by a world of continuing change.

In devising service projects for work in the Negro community itself, we must be careful to work only as enablers. It is often far more difficult to recruit, train and stimulate others to do a task than it is to do it ourselves. Yet, when we perform a task in the stead of others, several limiting things happen. When our work stops, there is no self-generating agency to continue where we left off. Then again, when only our hands have been put to work, the multiplied resources which we might have equipped for self-generating or self-directed service do not produce their multiplied results. Enabling work should be done with those who will or should have the responsibility for the work's continuation. Thus we begin and end with would-be responsible adults. Effective ways of recruiting, stimulating, training and initially sustaining adults in new tasks which they should routinely assume need to be devised and taught to large numbers of those who wish to serve as enablers. Older young people, as well as adults, can do this. They can share in visiting with local people from door to door, and in other unobtrusive ways alerting, informing and encouraging those who need such support in their efforts toward common goals.

Negroes need to be assisted in efforts to organize themselves. There are enabling ways in which all may share in this kind of endeavor. The need for such organization is urgent. Divisiveness in any portion of a community works to the detriment of all. In every benighted community such division can be costly. The Negro community—the most long benighted in America—is no exception to this rule. Divisiveness in the Negro community creates waste for which all must pay. We may therefore choose whether we shall pay in a limited way for prevention or pay continually for effects. In reference to the need for organization in the Negro community, the late Dr. Adam Clayton Powell, Sr., wrote:

> The race was completely disorganized when the Emancipation Proclamation was issued. At the close of the Civil War, there were as many groups and factions as there were slave plantations. These groups were not only taught by their owners to mistrust and hate each other, but the members of each group also were encouraged to tattle on each other. This was necessary to maintain the institution of slavery.[2]

When others outside the Negro community see the need for organization among Negroes, they often tend to see no more than what the late Dr. Powell has related here. But the Powell statement goes on to speak of how the Negro people have been organized by the Negro churches and other agencies. These organizations need, however, to be brought together to serve the economic and civic purposes which can be achieved through Negro solidarity and self-respect. Organization for these purposes cannot be done directly by anyone other than Negroes themselves. In this vein Dr. Powell explained: "I do not consider the . . . NAACP and the National Urban League, Negro organizations. These organizations for the most part are supported by white people and largely dominated by them." Negroes definitely must belong to these organizations, bringing even greater resources to them than in the past. Still, by far the most basic and as yet unaccomplished task lies in the fact that Negroes must organize themselves. In this endeavor they must begin by utilizing substantial resources supplied by others, in terms of brain power, money, and quietly unobtrusive time-absorbing facilitating tasks. The very divisiveness of Negroes ironically makes massive financial and other support from the white community an initial catalyzing necessity. The important continuing ingredients are Negro leadership, self-determination and growing financial self-support of the organization designed for developing self-respect. Organization gives to the Negro an equitable power stance from which to treat with dignity those outside of his own community. All of America can benefit from this. Its tangible encouragement is an immediately vital necessity in every community in the land.

The churches of America have begun to encourage such organization among Negroes. Principles of the Community Organization for Development, or C.O.D., for the northeastern New Jersey Negro and Spanish-speaking communities, need to be widely disseminated and discussed. White people of all age groups and of all levels of influence may be involved in C.O.D.-

type enterprise in many new forms of service, devised freshly to meet each need or situation as it may arise.

In whatever service the churches perform in regard to the Negro community, the churches may grow only as they are first willing to be changed themselves. Oppressors cannot truly help the oppressed in enduring and growth-producing ways. Our mindset may be changed for an openness to truly creative service only as we first disavow and disassociate ourselves from the privileges of being white. We must make interraciality into a two-way street, facilitating the opportunity of those whom we would serve—and others like them—to have access to all the same advantages and to all the same relationships as are open and available to us. Otherwise we work in limited and self-defeating ways which frustrate our national purposes, and we as churchmen deny the basic realities of the church's inner life.

Sacred Possibilities

The concept of Black Power directly involves a forthright claim to the inherent dignity and worth of black people. Life does have worth, and that worth is realized when it has or appropriates the power to become what it should be. Such power as this is inherently religious, and it points to a neglected aspect of religious life in the churches of America.

The earliest Christian creed addressed itself to the issue of power. It simply spoke of Jesus as Lord. In the cultural context in which the first creed was uttered it was an affirmation and commitment to Jesus as the divine embodiment and expression of power. Power as God's breath, according to the Genesis story of the creation, was infused into the life of man. Man was thereby given the potential likeness of his Creator. He was made to live in time as he would live in eternity.

In both symbolic and literal terms in the Hebrew-Christian religious experience, all that God's power touches is said to be sacred. To be sacred means to have an eternal dimension. It means to reflect the power, or to fulfill the purposes, of God. To the precise extent that Black Power affirms and extends God's truth and purposes, it is in that same degree possessed of a sacred and eternal nature. It is partially thus a sign of the presence of God's rule, which is what is meant by the term "the kingdom of God."

Philosophically, life does not move upward toward the end of time. Time and eternity are not time sequences. Life does not historically improve as time goes on. There is always conflict, and never in the broadest sense is there "enduring peace." Time and eternity are like two horizontal though infinitely unequal lines, which are close enough to be in a kind of tension. Wherever the power of the eternal is appropriated and realized in human life, at such precise points the lines of time and eternity converge and become as one. Thus God's power may always be appropriated. We may at any time enter into, accept, and fulfill our divine and eternal inheritance "in Christ." Life in the kingdom, under God's rule and in His power, is an ever-present immediate possibility. The sacred is anything which at any point in the time-eternity complex is God-empowered or God-possessed.

In a religious sense, then, the expression of human dignity, as in the term Black Power, speaks to immediately present possibilities, as one chooses to merge his life with the purposes and qualities of life lived on the level of the eternal. It is this sense of the presence of the eternal which the apocalyptic literature of the Old Testament sought to add to the judgmental sense of prophecy. So often in the churches our social concerns unhelpfully annoy, as those who teach of other-directed duties take on something of the demeanor of or are seen as God's angry men. There is an absence of a sense that there is always present the power to make sacred purposes immediate realities.

The apocalyptic literature is marked by involvement of the things of the eternal with the things of time. Time and eternity converge. The Prophet Elisha's experience of looking into the heavens and seeing the hosts of heaven coming to his rescue and prompting the observation that "They who are with us are more than they who are against us" (II Kings 6:16), is an example of the apocalyptic. The appearances of angelic or heavenly beings in the Genesis literature, the experience of Daniel in the lion's den, the deliverance at the Red Sea, and the deliverance from the fiery furnace—all, in a sense, are examples of at least the spirit of the apocalyptic.

The apocalyptic sees in immediate terms the vindication of the ultimate plans and programs and purposes of God. Its art or grace is the capacity to look through the mind's eye into the heavens and to see from heaven's perspective what we may recognize as being actualized on an eternal plane. What is to come to pass is, even now, on an eternal plane.

What the apocalyptic adds to the judgmental sense of prophecy is the dimension not simply of confidence of ultimate vindication. It adds, more significantly, the grace to seek to enter *in immediate terms* into the experience of the realities (or goals) which are yet to be. It makes the so-called "art of the possible" either obsolete or else redefines it to include the ultimate.

A prophetic concern allows for—and makes acceptable—the sounding of the trumpets. The apocalyptic adds the imperative— and the grace—to reshape our own involvement in present affairs as though the ultimate were either a present or proximate fact. Those who are concerned with human dignity or with any aspect of the divine purpose may here see how with quiet confidence we may boldly enter into new and sacred dimensions of life with immediacy, with graciousness and command. It is in this spirit that black men may walk, even now, revealing each day something of the power which comes from eternity. Seeing this, others doubtless will wish to appropriate this same power and walk with them . . . forever.

The Black Power concept presents itself as an opportunity for the churches of America. In many ways it may raise new questions and suggest possibilities for the quickening of a self-awareness in the churches of the land. This might be akin to the arousing of a giant possessed of infinite strength of which he had been unaware.

X

The Difficulties of Self-Awareness

In a discussion concerning Black Power one participant asked whether it might not be wise simply not to use the term Black Power. In its place, so he suggested, there might be spelled out the specific needs of Negroes for better housing, more jobs, quality education, and various civil rights.

Of course, there are other terms which might be used to indicate various aspects of Black Power, as has been the case throughout this book. Nonetheless, the suggestion overlooks the most important need of black people, and one to which the term Black Power speaks in a clear and direct way. The black people of America most pointedly need power. Above all else they need the power for self-realization, to become themselves in all of the inherent possibilities which this signifies for the Negro's own good and for larger the good of the whole nation. Only as all Americans become the best that they can be can America become its total best. What is true of individuals in personal terms is true also of groups, where groups as such relate to the nation's life.

Past Images

Negroes have had many images of themselves. This is true of all people and groups. But every group—as does every person—

tends to develop an image of itself that is marked by the greatest sense of worth and dignity. Thus the Jews have seen themselves as the descendants of Abraham who had made a covenant with God. The Irish of the last century, although plagued with famine, had what was to many of them the sure and in some degree sustaining knowledge or belief that they were the direct descendants of kings. Every Scotsman knows that there were never horse-thieves among his forebears, that they were all, without exception, the most exemplary of men. People develop mythologies which—along with some measure of truth—help preserve their sense of dignity. Negroes, no less than any other ethnic group, have tended to place a high value upon themselves. Yet the peculiar circumstances of the Negro in America over the past several centuries have led the Negro to develop the appearance of viewing himself in ways that deprecate his own sense of inherent worth. For simple survival during America's period of youthful insecurity, the Negro had to accommodate himself to the nation's adolescence. He thus assumed outwardly the only role by which his life could be sustained, taking on the appearance of accepting himself as a person of inferior worth.

We are familiar, through the defensively inspired lore of the youthful nation's developing but as yet uncertain mind, with stories of Uncle Remus and Uncle Tom. The unwritten job descriptions of Negroes, who wanted the secure means for livelihood, included for generations the assuming of an attitude of servility, buffoonery, or obsequiousness. In some degree the enforced role-playing became a part of the cultural stance of black people. In a sense, it offered a saving relief from otherwise unbearable tension. Nonetheless there was a built-in tendency toward rebellion. For Negroes, however outwardly degraded, were still men with the common human estimate of their own unique self-worth.

Negroes are a peculiarly American hybrid. But they have been taught to think of themselves in terms of the African portion of their ancestry alone. Although European and Indian by blood in part, and chiefly European in terms of culture, Negroes have been forced to develop a self-image which reflects a primary identification with their peculiarly African past. Thus the American Negro's initial self-image was associated with his experience on African soil. Apparently the vast majority of Negroes who came or were originally transported to America—in the 17th and 18th centuries—were of what we could call a tremendously high calibre. The native cultures from which large numbers of Negroes were taken to be slaves afforded a sense of human dignity, for the so-called average man and for those at the bottom of the socioeconomic pyramid, relatively greater than did the then prevailing cultures of Europe. The accounts of the capturing and transporting of Negro slaves are filled with evidences of the pride of station and the refusal to submit to the degradation of slavery. That often most of the slaves died was due apparently more to the will of the slaves than to the savage cruelty of their captors; and this is evidence of a self-concept which speaks of dignity and worth. Many of the captives deliberately ate large quantities of mud, a feat calculated to inflict upon themselves sure death. No fate was worse to them than slavery.

The Negroes who did arrive in the Americas were, quite often, of at least as high a station and relative cultivation as the white Americans among whom they came to work as slaves. We tend traditionally to think of Negroes as early accepting the place in life which the dominant American culture had assigned to them, and as holding a self-concept consistent with it. That this was not wholly true is evidenced by one bit of writing of an 18th-century female slave, Phillis Wheatley, who later secured her freedom.

Phillis Wheatley was born in Africa, probably in the year 1753, and was brought to Boston when she was about eight years old. There she served as a maid for a tailor, John Wheatley, and his wife. The Wheatleys taught Phillis how to read. Within 16 months of her arrival—having never heard the English language before leaving her native land—she had mastered the language to such an extent that the most difficult passages of the Bible were relatively easy to her. At the age of 13 Phillis Wheatley began to write poetry, and before her death in 1784, at the age of 31, she had written 39 books of poetry and become one of the then few women authors in the world. Her poetry was memorized for more than a generation by children in the South, as well as the North, as they read the "Prymers" by which the elements of the English language were taught the young.

Phillis Wheatley reflected in one poem in particular a sense of graciousness and judgment with reference to white Americans, along with a high concept of self-worth, which might be taken as no isolated phenomenon for the Negroes of her time. Her simple words have something of a compelling appeal. She writes:

> 'Twas mercy brought me from my *Pagan* land,
> Taught my benighted soul to understand
> That there's a God, that there's a Saviour, too;
> Once I redemption neither sought nor knew.
> Some view our sable race with scornful eye
> "Their colour is a diabolical dye."
> Remember, Christians, Negroes black as Cain,
> May be refin'd, and join the angelic train.

Such are the words of Phillis Wheatley. She reflected a self-image of dignity, refinement, and worth.

While Uncle Remus and Uncle Tom images of the Negro have been painted by non-Negro authors for the dominant white community, Negroes have always tended to feel differently about themselves. There has been, by and large, no difference in any age in the Negro's conception of himself. He has, for practical reasons of bread and butter, not given as much public expression to it in some circumstances as in others. This is crucial to our understanding of some of the current problems attendant to the Negro's coming into his own and for an appreciation of the efforts of the Negro both for increased communication and community with those around him.

We may look at another example of how the Negro has felt about himself, as expressed in the thought of one who was doubtless the foremost Negro leader of 100 years ago, the abolitionist Frederick Douglass. Frederick Douglass was born in 1817 and died in 1895. His life thus spanned the century in which the basic legal issue of freedom and slavery was fought. He has been said to have symbolized the indomitable will and determination to realize the fullness of human dignity in the minds of the 19th-century American Negro. Douglass was, incidentally, viewed by his contemporaries as one of the greatest orators of his century. In the mid-1800s he spoke with a frank clarity words which not only bear significance in reference to the Negro's self-concept, but are reflective of a broad principle which must be borne in mind in every effort based upon goodwill toward those who appear to be less fortunate than ourselves. Douglass wrote: "No people that has solely depended on foreign aid, or rather, upon the efforts of those, in any way identified with the oppressor, to undo heavy burdens ever stood forth in the attitude of freedom."

Again he wrote that "the man who has *suffered the wrong* is the man to demand *redress*—that the man *struck* is the man to cry out—and he who has *endured the cruel pangs of Slavery is the man to advocate Liberty.*"

Douglass never advocated unilateral action, conceiving as he did the human race to be one in the deepest sense of the term. His emphasis upon self-determination, self-direction, and self-help, however, is here made unmistakably clear.

In the past, while Negroes often have had to grin, to focus their eyes on the ground, and to shuffle their feet in the presence of white people, there has been on their part an unmistakable strain toward the highest sense of human dignity and worth.

Social Significance

Negroes thus have had forced upon them a divided image of of themselves. Such a state of things is always fraught with per-

sonal and social peril. The kind of schizophrenia foisted upon
the Negro has reflected in more basic ways the split personality
of American life. It is a personality pattern of long standing and
continues to be inadequately confronted even today.

The psychosis occasioned by America's failure to resolve the
tension of mutually antagonistic commitments has its adverse
affects not only in relation to the Negro, but also in other areas
of the nation's life. Our national failure, for example, to come
to terms with the as yet insufficiently publicized scandal of farm
subsidy, which has long served no fundamental need and yet is
an ever-widening open drain upon the nation's financial resources,
reveals something of America's split personality, the effects of
which pervade the nation's life.

The National Committee of Negro Churchmen, in a meeting
held marking the 80th anniversary of the Statue of Liberty, addressed themselves to the evidences of this state of national psychosis. Their statement declared in part:

> We submit that to pass a Civil Rights Bill as this nation
> did in 1875 and then refuse to enforce it; to pass another
> Civil Rights Bill (weaker this time) in 1964 and then refuse
> to enforce it; to begin an anti-poverty program with insuffi-
> cient funds in the first place and then to put the lion's share
> of this miniscule budget into Head Start programs when un-
> employment among Negro men continues to sky-rocket; to
> declare segregation in our schools unconstitutional as the
> Supreme Court did in 1954, and then refuse to end it forth-
> with; to set up guidelines for desegregating hospitals and
> then refuse to appropriate moneys for the enforcement of
> these guidelines; to insist on civil rights legislation aimed at
> the south and then to defeat the first piece of such legisla-
> tion relevant to areas outside the south; to preach "law and
> order" into the anguish of Negro slums in full view of the
> contributions of policemen to that anguish and then to
> insist that policemen be their own judges; to hear the sub-
> urban politicians declaim against open occupancy in one
> breath and in the very next breath insist that they are not

racists: These are the ironies which stare us in the face and
make it all but impossible to talk about how much "progress" has been made. The fact of the matter is if black
Americans are not accorded basic human and constitutional
rights which white Americans gain immediately upon their
entry into citizenship, then there really are no substantive
gains of which to speak.

The nation cannot continue to be divided with the depth and
pervasiveness that its long-standing personality pattern reveals
and build at the same time for wholeness and integrity in any
aspect of its life. Doubtless the divisions which often seem to be
but superficial between American political parties in no small
measure are a reflection of the basic antagonisms which strain
at the very foundations of the nation's life. The cancerous disease
of racism cannot run rampant and still allow the political, economic, intellectual, social, and spiritual fabric of the nation to
be other than diseased. The most secure focus on—and therefore
the best approach to—the malignancy which frustrates wisdom
and efficiency in government and destroys a singleness of purpose
which would make for integrity in thought and action may be
found in the area of race relations in America today. It is
the American attitude toward what it sees as the color question which dims our nation's vision of reality, creating an illusory
world of make-believe, in which we blindly stumble, insensitive
to the deadly precipice which lies not too far ahead.

The fact that America, as a whole, fails to see its Negro population in terms of reality is clear evidence of a national debilitation. This comes about from a natural tendency not to see others
whose presence confronts us with personal or moral dilemmas.
Thus it is that the Negro is in human terms at once America's
most highly visible and yet most unperceived reality. This suggests
that if and as we come to accept the fact that the black people
of America cannot be wished away, we may grow and develop
more readily in our capacity to face other aspects of human
reality. The black people of America are here to stay. They are

an indelible part of the lives of all who comprise America. They truly are the most unique hybrid of the melting pot. They have added to America's economic wealth, and are demanding more incessantly than any other group in America to be allowed to add to the nation's integrity and fulfillment in every area of the nation's life.

As we as individuals and as a nation come to see and accept the Negro part of the nation's life, which is an interrelated aspect of each of us in America, we may mature in our own personal and national self-image. We may thus come as individuals to see more clearly our present friends and our families, and hopefully also may perhaps even come to see and know what is potentially the most threatening of all—ourselves.

It was Hughes Mearns who, a generation ago, wrote the famous quatrain which goes to the heart of the problem of our not seeing what we would wish away:

> As I was walking up the stair,
> I met a man who wasn't there.
> He wasn't there again today.
> I wish, I wish he'd stay away.

How true this is of the American and of the human experience!

It may well be that the Negro's growing self-awareness, expressing itself in what is heard in seemingly threatening terms, may yet help to move America forward toward the greater sense of sanity and wholeness which it so desperately needs.

Recall to Commitments

It is fortunate for the nation that the same assertion of human dignity which gives voice to the pleas today for power for black people has continuously marked the Negro's life. The condition of Negroes has always served to recall America in some measure to its basic commitments to human freedom and fulfillment.

More than a century ago, when the persistent issue of Negro
freedom took a somewhat different form from what it does today,
Frederick Douglass asked white Americans to see themselves as
other Americans saw them. Speaking before a predominantly
white audience at Rochester, New York, on July 5, 1852, he
asserted:

> What to the American slave, is your 4th of July? I answer;
> a day that reveals to him, more than all other days in the
> year, the gross injustice and cruelty to which he is the con-
> stant victim. To him your celebration is a sham; your
> boasted liberty, an unholy license; your national greatness
> swelling vanity; your denunciation of tyrants, brass fronted
> impudence; your shouts of liberty and equality, hollow
> mockery; your prayers and hymns, your sermons and thanks-
> givings, with all your religious parade and solemnity, are to
> him, more bombast, fraud, deception, impiety, and hypoc-
> risy—a thin veil to cover up crimes which would disgrace
> a nation of savages . . .

This same aggressive sense of manhood and dignity which gave
utterance to such a challenge to America has tended to persist
throughout the Negro's history. It was evidenced in a compelling
way in the meeting of the National Committee of Negro Churchmen at the Statue of Liberty on November 3, 1966. In tones
echoing those of Frederick Douglass of more than a century ago,
and against the threat of November election backlash, the
churchmen declared:

> Our purpose here is neither to beg nor to borrow, but to
> state the determination of black men in America to exact
> from this nation not one whit less than our full manhood
> rights. We will not be cowed nor intimidated in the land of
> our birth. We intend that the truth of this country, as ex-
> perienced by black men, will be heard. We shall state this
> truth from the perspective of the Christian faith and in the

light of our experience with the Lord of us all in the bleak-
ness of this racially idolatrous land.

The statement of the churchmen clearly was not designed
basically to win friends, but to command respect. It has been
true of all rising ethnic groups in America that justice and equity
have been commanded out of each rising group's own sense of
dignity and worth. The churchmen thus asserted the Negro's
equal roots with other Americans, first as pilgrims and then as
enforced servants and as free men, in the nation's life. Perhaps
the most compelling aspect of the statement of their place in
American life was expressed in these poignant words:

> We remind Americans that in our beginnings we were all
> exiles, strangers sojourning in an unfamiliar land. Even the
> first black men who set foot on these shores came, as did
> most white men, in the role of pilgrims, not slaves. Sharing
> common aspirations and hopes for a land where freedom
> could take root and live, for the briefest of moments black
> men and white men found each other in a community of
> trust and mutual acceptance.
>
> However, if America became a "Mother of Exiles" for
> white men, she became at the same time a cruel system of
> bondage and inhumanity to black men. Far from finding
> here a maternal acceptance, her black sons were thrust into
> the depth of despair, at times so hopeless that it wrung from
> their lips the sorrow song: "Sometimes I feel like a mother-
> less child." What anguish is keener, what rejection more
> complete, or what alienation more poignant than this expe-
> rience which called for the metaphor, "motherless child"?
>
> But that is only part of our story. For somewhere in the
> depth of their experiences within this great land, those same
> black men and women found a ground of faith and hope
> on which to stand. Never accepting on the inside the identity
> forced upon them by a brutalizing white power, they also
> sang—even prior to emancipation—"Before I'll be a slave,
> I'll be buried in my grave and go home to my Lord and be

free." A faith of this quality and integrity remains alive today.

The current impetus toward Black Power reflects the same life-and-death faith and determination as expressed in these words of the Negro churchmen. White Americans should have no cause to fear the Negro's determination to have America become what it must be. Freedom and human dignity for all Americans spell only a fuller and richer life for all.

The statement of the churchmen at the Statue of Liberty emphasized the continuing halting between opposing opinions which historically has characterized the nation's life. The churchmen held that it is this continuing dilemma which has created our present racial crisis. It involves a crisis of commitment. At this point the statement explained:

> There is, to be sure, a continuing dilemma of "crisis and commitment" in our country. But, it is not the quarrels among the civil rights leaders, nor is it the debate about Black Power, nor is it the controversy surrounding the riots in our cities. The crisis is what it has always been since shortly after the first black Americans set foot upon these shores. It is not a crisis rooted in the Negro community. It is a "crisis of commitment" among white Americans who have consistently taken two steps forward toward becoming mature men on race and one and a half steps backward at the same time. The power of the "New Colossus" has never been fully committed to eliminating this monstrous racism from the life of the American people.

The Role of Riots

The current growing self-awareness of the black people of America has led them to place not only the crisis in philosophical terms at the feet of white Americans. Negroes have placed there as well the roots of the riots which have brought growing night-mares to our city streets.

From one point of view the riots may be seen as a logical result of the historic stunting or distorting of the Negro's self-image. He has been allowed openly to think of himself only as an adolescent, half-grown man. He has been locked in the role of one who would grow into manhood and self-sufficiency but has been firmly held in check. We know what difficulties inevitably arise when growth out of adolescence is ever thwarted. In terms of the results of a simple and long-continued thwarting of growth into maturity and manhood, the irrationality of the recent riots could be more than sufficiently explained. The wonder is, so Dr. Kenneth Clark has suggested, that there have been so few riots.

Another related view is that the Negro has long been taught to hate himself. The riots reflect a self-image of hatred. They represent self-inflicted punishment on the Negro community itself. They have involved thus far at least in their death and destruction only the Negro community. Still another, and similarly related, estimate of the riots suggests that the Negro's irrationality will tend for a time to increase as the Negro makes his long-postponed exit from half-maturity into manhood. Thus we are counselled to deal with the Negro's growth into adulthood and self-directed maturity in much the same manner as we would deal with any growth out of adolescence. We must understand it, and we must face it creatively and sympathetically. There is no other positive and growth-facilitating way ahead. To clamp a tight lid on adolescent groping after maturity is to invite violence to human life and to create social dynamite. On the other hand, unlimited permissiveness is equally destructive. The period of change from adolescence to maturity calls for increased com-munication, appreciation, facilitation, and ample room for the natural expression of both the rational and seemingly irrational hostilities which mark this critical period of human growth.

That Negroes have had apparently more than suffucent cause for latent hostilities should be evident to all. The nation has long denied its Negro citizens the basic freedom and opportunity which all Americans are due. It must be expected that these hostilities will be vented. The November 3, 1966, statement of the National Committee of Negro Churchmen at the Statue of Liberty spoke to this situation in these words:

> Look at the record of fitful and mincing steps forward and of cowardly steps away from the goal of racial justice. The slaves were freed in 1863, but the nation refused to give them land to make that emancipation meaningful. Simultaneously, the nation was giving away millions of acres in the midwest and west—a gift marked "for whites only." Thus an economic floor was placed under the new peasants from Europe, but for America's oldest peasantry was provided only an abstract freedom. In the words of Frederick Douglass, emancipation made the slaves "free to hunger; free to the winter and rains of heaven . . . free without roofs to cover them or bread to eat or land to cultivate . . . ! We gave them freedom and famine at the same time. The marvel is that they still live."
>
> We should, therefore, be neither shocked nor surprised that our slums today confront us with the bitter fruits of that ancient theft. Is it conceivable that the shrill cry "Burn, Baby, Burn" in Watts, Los Angeles, and across this country, could ever be invented by men with reasonable chances to make a living, to live in a decent neighborhood, to get an adequate education for their children? Is it conceivable that men with reasonable prospects for life, liberty, and the pursuit of happiness for themselves and for their children could ever put the torch to their own main streets? The answer is obvious. These are the anguished, desperate acts of men, women, and children who have been taught to hate themselves and who have been herded and confined like cattle in rat-infested slums.
>
> Frederick Douglass is indeed correct when he suggests that "the marvel is that Negroes are still alive," not to mention sane.

Negroes are angry. This is an evidence of their being human. Any normal man would be. Yet Negroes have resorted almost wholly to peaceable means in their calling for a redress of their wrongs. What greater evidence of faith in our way of life has been given by any segment of American life?

Whom Shall We Trust?

The widespread increase of self-awareness among Negroes has led to new perceptions of relationships both within and without the Negro community. It has led to the current recognition on the part of black Americans of the truth expressed more than a century ago by Frederick Douglass that he who is oppressed must himself speak to the oppressor. There is the conviction abroad that only self-respect and self-development may command the respect of others. At the same time Negroes are impatient with the "tried and true" paths, which have not issued in an effective closing of the gap between where Negroes and white people are in every aspect of the nation's life.

What black people are now saying increasingly to their traditional benefactors comes through at times as effrontery. They are saying in effect that only if white Americans work with black Americans out of mutual self-interest and a perceived mutuality of involvement will they take the hand of mutually reinforcing help. As to the ostensible charity of white people, there is the feeling that what white Americans have had to give has come about in no inconsiderable part from their enjoyment of opportunities from which Negroes were excluded and which were due to be shared by all. Negroes would hold that they are not asking for charity, but for some measure of just restitution and equity in immediate terms at all levels of American life. Thus white leaders who have been paternalistically kind, who feel that they know better than Negroes themselves what is good for Negroes and who have no sense of lively guilt for their small or large part in sharing the spoils of the Negro's inheritance—these white leaders are being rejected. Other white leaders, in what are seen to be largely Negro affairs, are increasingly being asked to assist in enabling ways rather than to lead.

At the same time, those promoting in thoughtful ways the needed impetus toward Black Power have tended to call for solidarity among Negroes, despite their inevitable differences. Thus specifically the National Committee of Negro Churchmen, while not labelling itself as a Black Power group, but clearly recognizing the need for power for black people, has called for general support for leaders of diverse approaches to the empowerment of the powerless black people of America. The churchmen declared on November 3, 1966: "We support all our civil rights leaders for we believe that they all have important insights to share with us on this critical question." Negroes committed to progress cannot afford the luxury of criticizing other leaders. They are all, hardly without exception, in some degree mutually re-enforcing. Speaking of the immediate goal before Negro Americans, they continued:

> For our part, we submit that our basic goal in this struggle is to make it possible for all persons and groups to participate with power at all levels of our society. Integration is not an aesthetic goal designed to add token bits of color to institutions controlled entirely by whites. Integration is a political goal with the objective of making it possible for Negroes and other Americans to express the vitality of their personal and group life in institutions which fundamentally belong to all Americans.

In this endeavor the leadership of Negroes is being encouraged. That the Negro has been looked upon as less than a man is no recent phenomenon. Emasculation of the Negro began in slavery, when only a smiling mammy could state clearly to white Americans the feelings of black Americans. Black Americans are realizing that their growth into positive self-awareness is needed for the attainment of any reasonable measure of self-directed self-sufficiency. Black Americans need the power of self-realization. Others cannot bring this about for them. They can help, however, in many enabling ways. It is for the good of all in America that this should and must be done.

There are, as we have suggested, many hazards which come as the price for the self-awareness which will lead to maturity for Negroes, and so hopefully in a much needed way for all of America. We must expect from Negroes often an awkward self-assertion, and at as many times an equally awkward and halting retreat by white people from previous positions of presumed superiority. We must expect that many Negroes will assume that simply being black makes Negroes omni-competent. In this they will simply be aping, in possibly more immediately ludicrous ways, the empty arrogance of their white mentors in this regard. Yet black Americans must come to know that black ignorance is no antidote to nor an effective positive substitute for white oppression.

Not insignificant among the difficulties which will be occasioned by the growing self-awareness among Negroes will be the embarrassment of many white business leaders and leaders of other institutions who come face to face, perhaps for the first time, with their evident past patterns of racial prejudgment and discrimination. As self-awareness in Negroes catalyzes their visibility in the white community, every institution in our society will become painfully aware of overlooked resources which could have been used with substantial profit for themselves and for others.

The large numbers of Negroes in the greatest poverty will doubtless press for change in ways harder than our normal social processes would encourage. Their pressures will need to be accepted and facilitated with the fullest possible resources, if chaos is not to deepen. As we come to see their needs as both legitimate and long overdue, we shall tend to be open to the urgent basic change and adaptations which their conditions demand. Further, and perhaps most important. the substantial changes which will be of benefit to the urban Negro poor must be of such a character as to benefit both business and society as a whole in long-range terms. The black poor want immediate solutions of a substantial nature which are both sound for America as a whole and for its business life. Negroes who are poor do not want costly palliatives which in the long run are to the benefit of none.

Perhaps the greatest difficulty which the new sense of self-awareness on the part of black Americans will create is in the area of leadership roles and in the taking of initiative. In a way, as with adults who have seen or thought of others as children, it will tend to be awkward for many, if not most, white people to hear Negroes speaking to whites as man to man, and even as their guides. Most white people, including those who are kindly disposed, have tended to think of Negroes as children of a kind. Yet the new stance which Negroes will be taking is what is needed for America; and black men who are already self-aware are determined to give to America both graciously and forthrightly all that their hitherto largely unused resources will allow. In this regard, let us listen to the words of the Negro churchmen in their meeting before the Statue of Liberty:

> Let us try to be very clear about one thing, America. Black Americans are determined to have all of their full human and constitutional rights. We will not cease to agitate this issue with every means available to men of faith and dignity until justice is done.
>
> We are dealing at bottom with a question of relationship between black and white, between rich and poor, ultimately between believers in different gods . . . To this end, we of the Negro church call for a massive mobilization of the resources in the Negro community in order to give leadership in the fulfillment not only of our own destiny but in order to help produce a more sane white America . . .
>
> Finally, we say to the American people, white and black, there is no turning back of the clock of time . . . America is at the crossroad. Either we become the democracy we can become, or we tread the path to self-destruction.

That the black people of America are growing into a new self-awareness is clearer day by day. That difficulties will be occasioned by the new relationships of power created by a growing self-awareness on the Negro's part also seems certain. Some of the difficulties will be fraught with pain and possible peril. Yet America has always had some measure of growing pains. It has always been a growing and maturing nation. The bearing of the pain such as will be occasioned by the Negro's own self-directed thrust into the mainstream of American life should, in itself, therefore be only a familiar and promising part of the basic American growth-producing tradition and experience.

XI

Is Brotherhood Enough?

The Limits of Altruism

Rather than working to empower life to become in self-directed ways what it should be, so often we have worked for what we have termed "brotherhood" instead. Brotherhood involves a lively sense of goodwill and understanding of the kind which we have promoted and exercised increasingly in America over the past generation. The question of the sufficiency of brotherhood as a continuing goal, however, in the face of the growing unrest in cities is one which needs to be asked urgently and repeatedly.

Daily throughout urban America there are fresh signs that all is not well for America as a whole. We are brought face to face with evidences of the mounting frustration of black masses crying out for the power to be free. Their current cries have been increasingly strange, sometimes uncouth, sometimes unnerving and unearthly. Seasoned with a new and peppery touch of "Whitey must go!," and now stirred by a threatening Black Panther, the inner city's atmosphere is one of increasingly pervasive pain marked by uneven ripples of revulsion and resignation.

The sense of revolt and revulsion, however distasteful, has about it a reasonable air; it expresses the irrationality of rational men who have seen themselves as pushed near to the point of

174

distraction. It is in itself an ironic sign of hope, an evidence of the innate sense of humanity of a people protesting man's perhaps unconscious, but no less unreasoning, callous inhumanity to those about him. The sense of seeming resignation among large numbers in our inner cities has an eerie and even more disconcerting air; it is marked by a feeling of the unreal. How can some human beings simply vegetate or live near to the level of the lower animals?

A walk through the bleak tenements, or, perhaps better, a stay there for a day and a night, would prove to be an unforgettable reminder that some in America are disinherited from the day of their birth. Here are people seemingly impotent in the face of signs of power everywhere. Yet we are coming to know that no man, woman or child is ever wholly impotent. There are always latent powers, either slowly budding or potentially explosive powers, powers ready to be harnessed to purposes which are either good or ill. They may be used for America's growth and for the good of all. Or they may serve to invest the growing unrest in our city streets with the capacity for national calamity.

It is against a background such as this that I must inescapably look at the prospects for the near future of America. In our family there are five children, four of them ranging in age from twenty-four to sixteen, and then there is the little ruler of our household, young Carolyn, age seven. I reflect upon the fact that in forty more years I shall be no more in this land of the living. I tend to think of our older children as being somewhat self-sufficient and self-directing. But sentimentalist that I am, and intrigued by the bright-eyed hopefulness of a seven-year old, I daily become more deeply and acutely concerned about the kind of world which those of my generation will bequeath to her and to those like her. The difficulty of the problem is compounded when I recognize that with all of the good family life which we may try to provide and with all the graces for growth which may be bestowed upon her—along with our other children—she and her brothers and sisters may yet come to inhabit what may be for all who are of their generation an almost utterly uninhabitable world.

In spite of all of our post-World War II efforts toward brother-hood and toward the acceptance of our Carolyn's kind into the mainstream of American life, by many signs the hard realities appear to say that the gap between where Negroes are on the one hand, and all other Americans are on the other, is not diminish-ing. In the midst of all of our well-intentioned efforts at a past and present goodwill, a great gulf seems steadily and surely com-ing to be fixed in America at least between the majority of our society and its largest racial minority.

There can be little doubt that the most imminent peril facing us as a nation today lies in the growing isolation and awareness of a lack of worth and place in America on the part of its Negro minority.

One fact apparent to many Americans, including Negroes of education and some degree of affluence, is that daily new op-portunities hitherto unknown to Negro Americans are being opened for our Negro minority. It is clear also that, with the Civil Rights Act of 1964, the greatest declared weight of the federal government in nearly 100 years was given to the goal of the secur-ing of the Negro's place more nearly in the center of American life. Thus to the understandable perceptions of many, if not most, Americans, there have been more than sufficient facts to support the daily working assumption that progress is being made in improving the Negro's lot.

Yet these perceptions are not shared by the masses of Negro poor. Their daily awareness is of a growing sense of poverty, of increasing deprivation, of widening isolation, and of mounting frustration, as opportunities for more than simple survival remain largely closed to them. Their feelings square with what the eco-nomic facts of their situation reveal. There is, indeed, an unclos-ing gap between what Negroes have on the one hand and what their white counterparts—circumstance by circumstance—have on the others. Nor is there evidence that any of our major efforts toward a betterment of the Negro's lot in relation to that of

America as a whole are paying off in the way that most of us would hope and have believed they would.

In our central cities where the majority of our nation's Negroes live, poverty is mounting, as survival costs for rent and food and life's bearest necessities increasingly tend to overtake and to exceed the subsistence wages and welfare grants available to our Negro poor. Made-work in our most recent public efforts at the abolition of poverty, however efficient it may be in some instances, moves on almost of necessity at such a slow pace that the surface of the problem is scarcely scratched. And all the while the sense of hopelessness of the poor caught in the goalless grind of their daily ghetto life broods over our central cities like an ever-darkening shadow. And our Negro poor know that while made-work may feed a hungry mouth today, it holds no secure promise for tomorrow or for the days which may yet lie beyond.

By new signs coming to the forefront at practically every hand, we shall be recalled from our past and present dreams of progress in American so-called race relations. This much is almost certain. We shall be reminded of this, if not by government statistics and other clear evidences showing the Negro's diminishing proportion of the American good life, then by the unleashed hostility of the Negro poor themselves.

The American Negro is aware that he has an educational and skills deficiency, that he needs more and newer types of education to fit him for greater utility in the increasingly technologically oriented employment market. Yet he knows that, even where such training may be available, the overwhelming odds are still against him. Only a little more than one-fourth of the disparity between non-white and white family income is due to the Negro's having less education. The bulk of the disparity is due to other causes.

Is our past and present goal of brotherhood, then, enough? Can we afford the luxury of continuing to do the same kind of things in terms of our efforts toward equity and toward brotherhood as we have done in the past? The hard realities would seem to suggest that the immensity of the problem has to an almost frightening degree far outweighed what hindsight tells us are our well-intentioned but all-too-inadequate approaches to the realization of the national fulfillment which we really seek.

To ascertain clearly where we should go from here, we must perhaps first answer afresh the age-old question, "Am I my brother's keeper?" Human nature and the answer which had been given in the question's original biblical context suggest that man is never adequately motivated in his relationships with others, save in terms which take into consideration some degree of his own self-interest. Cain, to whom the classic question was addressed as to his being his brother's keeper, had already slain his brother Abel.

Our efforts in regard to the Negro in America have in the past been motivated ostensibly out of our concern for the Negro in and of himself. As such, it may be that our national efforts in regard to the Negro's welfare over the past years is to be seen as an enduring memorial to the well-nigh sublime goodwill and altruistic and non-self-interested concern on the part of the American white citizenry for those whom they have largely conceived as being other than their own.

In this sense, we may have reached a saturation point in regard to a people's capacity to do good almost solely in behalf of others. The assumption here is that personal and national self-interest must come to be seen as a foundation stone of our concern for the plight of black America. Those familiar with the religious literature of the Hebrew-Christian heritage will recognize that the appeal to self-interest provides the continuing sanction for its moral precepts.

The Use of Enlightened Self-Interest

In the light of this assumption, a possible clue to the future course of action which we should take may rest in the recognition that it is for the sake of America as a whole, and not simply for the sake of a major ethnic minority, that our efforts for fulfillment should be made. An approach such as this, from the Negro's point of view, would assuredly go far toward eliminating the paternalistic stance which goes so deeply against his grain.

At heart, what is suggested here is that the needs of black people in America must come to be seen as inseparable from the needs of the nation. Then possibly the current stagnation and abortiveness of our efforts toward improving the Negro's lot may be overcome; and so may the foundations for truly fruitful new endeavors at increasing the worthwhileness of the Negro's place in American life be made.

A few years ago one of the nation's foremost educators proposed to his board of education that possibly the most massive amount of money ever to be spent on an educational reconstruction program be invested in improving education in selected Negro areas of their city. The board members were overwhelmed. Pleas for economy were mixed with accusations of special group favoritism. To this the superintendent gave this reply: until extermination of the poor was made possible by law, no reasonable expense must be spared to remove them from the bonds of poverty.

Behind these terse and pointed remarks was the inescapable truth that either we must pay to develop all of our citizens for their fullest possible productiveness *and then give them every reasonable opportunity to produce* or we must pay the cost of their maintenance. The maintenance costs of the uneducated and idle poor are never ending. They include the burden of spiralling relief and policing services, the compounding of educational, health, sanitation and recreational problems, and the growth of illegitimacy and dependency with their mechanisms of self-stimulus and perpetuation. It has been said that the idled, unproductive poor are adept at and encouraged toward two tendencies for which only native skills are required; that is, to carouse and to reproduce. Those whom they produce tend to reproduce at earlier ages and in larger numbers than others in the population, so that their offspring reproduce often three generations in the space it normally takes for two. As the numbers of the idled and demoralized poor increase—as indeed they are increasing in the central cities of America—the burden to a largely white taxpaying public soars to ever new heights.

Birth control clinics have had little or no ascertainable effect upon those who are caught in the stultifying cycle of poverty and frustration. Life tends to lack a sense of purpose; and efforts toward discipline have a largely negative force. Education, opportunity and access to new relationships appear to be the only hope. More important, whatever may be the hope of our Negro poor must soon come to be seen as the only hope for the fulfillment of the life of our nation as a whole. Either we pay the calculated cost for the new mechanisms needed to empower people for self-directed self-sufficiency and for the creation of new opportunities and access to enabling relationships, or we must find ourselves facing two other self-defeating alternatives.

One alternative is to accept patiently the geometrically increasing and never-ending maintenance costs for the poor, by which we not only weary ourselves with taxation, but also tax mortgage the lives of our children and their children's children. This is the less deadly of the two self-defeating alternatives. The other is to let nature take its due collision course, with a growing mass of idled, angered, vice-ridden, untutored and highly visible and vocal poor coming face to face with a mounting lethargy and backlash such as our nation has never known. Where such a course might lead must rest with one's imagination. I shudder to think of its potential peril. Yet because I am concerned for my children—and for yours—and for the kind of world which we shall bequeath to them, I must—along with every other American—look realistically and soberly to the future to discern what it may hold. Then, in the light of what we see, each one of us must decide.

As to where I stand, I daily have less doubt.

Out of sheer self-interest, I know that I must face the fact,

however dismal and difficult it may seem to be, that our traditional efforts in regard to our black fellow-Americans of all economic and social levels have not been sufficient to provide for
my children and for yours the secure promise of hope for the
kind of world in which it shall be their lot to live. Those familiar
with the biblical literature will recognize the perennial need for
integrity on the part of responsible men who would make our
future safe. "If the trumpet sounds an unsure note," asked the
Apostle, "who shall prepare himself for the battle?"

Out of sheer self-interest, I am convinced that the people of
our nation must somehow be recalled from their useless dreams
that all is well. The only life I have I hope might be, with theirs,
directed along paths which lead not to destruction, but to peace
and fulfillment for all.

This same hope we all must hold for our families, our friends,
and for the world in which we live.

Self-interest prompts more than concern. It dictates a mind at
work by day and night sorting, weighing and spawning practical
first steps and beyond.

The Means of Hope

If brotherhood largely in terms of sentiment alone is not
enough, what can those of us both near to the problem and
seemingly less near do? We suggest in broad, but what we hope
may be helpful, terms four things, all of which are related to the
need for the equitable extension of power.

1—We can be open to radical possibilities for change. If our
minds are attuned to positive aspects of brotherhood, it is the nice
things that we shall see. If, on the other hand, we recognize the
need for new and more substantial approaches to a problem whose
dimensions are larger than we once thought, we shall be able to
appropriate and take advantage of new possibilities for basic
change when such come our way. One thing is certain. We can

never get the right answers if the true dimensions of the problem
are not defined. We have suggested in the foregoing pages that
the simplest keys to such answers as we seek are related to the
one word "power." How can we enable others to become what
they should be? As black people, we must settle for no less than
opportunities empowering us to become what we must be for
our own sake, and for that of our nation and our world.

2—We can make into practical priorities our theoretical concerns. All of us in America are in varying degrees committed to
the dream expressed in the *E Pluribus Unum* on our coins.
But the commitment all too often is but one among many. If we
are headed in the direction of peril, as our riots and the facts of
the hardening gulf bespeak, then we must come to put "first
things first." In our education enterprise, in our business affairs,
in our civic and religious life, we must find creative ways in
which the practicalities of equitable power use and extension may
be given a first consideration routinely day by day. The greatest
need and opportunity before America lies in the fullest appropriation of its unused human power for the good of all.

The poor, it has been said, will always be with us. This much
we can and must accept. But the problem of poverty lies not in
the fact that some men are poor. The problem of poverty comes
about when men do not have the power to develop and to fulfill
their potential to become, if their capacities so indicate, other
than arbitrarily poor. Everyone's having the power to fulfill his
potential means that some, in every generation and perhaps in
every household, will have richer possibilities than others. It
will mean that some will derive greater economic benefits than
others, but not as part of a class or as a race—or even a family.
For the children of the poor, when the potential of all is tapped
and fulfilled, may become what their talents decree.

More power to all! This must be our hope, our commitment,
and the end of our every endeavor. We must empower our restless and resentful black urban masses to make continuing and

self-directing changes, if the life of our cities is to be regenerated. Resources for urban rebuilding from without are wasted unless those who reside in our cities first are empowered for self-perpetuating improvement in the affairs of city life. Facilitation must therefore be given to the fullest development and expression of the latent power of the black urban masses.

This means that educators of every kind will work, in concert with our homes and our places of employment, to release talent, unafraid either of the neutralizing of the results of their work or of the hard fall which they have feared for those once seen to be disinherited. This means that industry—which has the greatest hope of immediate economic gain through an equitable power extension—may build in broader and more lasting supports for its free and competitive forms, once the talent of all is the most fully freed for the service of all. This means no less than greatness for our nation in every area of its life. The immediate commitment to equitable power extension may mean a new day in the nation's political life, as the empowering of those who must now walk rather than ride as they might is the ultimate dream of liberal and conservative alike. The power concept has been afforded us in the life of the black people of America at this hour in our nation's life.

Several clear choices are raised by the issue of Black Power in regard to our commitments. On the one hand, we may scoff at the power issue; we may decry it or simply wish it away. On the other hand, by seeing the significance of the power issue in terms of the good with which it may invest the nation at this immediately urgent hour we may be eternally thankful for it. In this spirit, we may take hold of the handle and use it for the largest good of all.

Thus the broad problems appearing as blemishes on the urban scene—and presently destined increasingly to touch the lives of all—may be the more effectively contained and, hopefully, done away with. The choice is ours. It speaks basically not to our altogether praiseworthy and notable altruism, but to the self-interest on the part of all which calls for our total commitment.

3—We can be steadfast in convincing others. News that is emotionally important to us we pass along. We do not let others either forget it or pass it by. For our children's sake, and for our own, we must let others know that we must work together not alone for the sake of the good of others, but also in a deeply personal, self-interested and self-empowering way for the kind of safe and secure and hope-filled world in which we would have our children live. Power must be harnessed for good purposes. It is never neutral. We must develop and direct all of America's power resources in self-conscious ways. This calls for the intelligent and continuing involvement of all who are a part of the nation's life.

4—Finally, we can commit ourselves to change. We cannot retain for ourselves the privileges of being white, and still make things better for the Negro poor. Every opportunity which we *have* had, *now* have or *may* have in the future—from which others had been denied consideration—means no less than that we ride to some extent on the backs of others. We cannot be change agents, unless we are willing to be changed ourselves. Black Americans must answer the challenge raised by the issue of Black Power by being changed most drastically themselves. They must move from dependence into independence. They must not ask what others have to give, but in forthright ways offer what latent rich gifts they have to bring the nation's life and their own lives to flower. In the strictest sense, the nation has never beckoned the impotent to rise. It has received those who have stood forth clearly with the offer of their power for the good of others. This must be the new posture of black Americans who would be free.

I look with hope to the future and believe that, for us and for all the children of our land, days of peace and power and fulfillment lie ahead. We may believe that this will be true for one good reason. We may be confident that every person truly concerned for the world in which we and our children live will hear and heed and take to heart and give his life to following along whatever paths that clear and compelling truth decrees. It is in this bright hope and sure confidence that these pages have been shared with you.

APPENDIX

"BLACK POWER"

A STATEMENT BY THE NATIONAL COMMITTEE OF NEGRO CHURCHMEN
July 31, 1966

We, an informal group of Negro churchmen in America, are deeply disturbed about the crisis brought upon our country by historic distortions of important human realities in the controversy about "black power." What we see shining through the variety of rhetoric is not anything new but the same old problem of power and race which has faced our beloved country since 1619.

We realize that neither the term "power" nor the term "Christian Conscience" is an easy matter to talk about, especially in the context of race relations in America. The fundamental distortion facing us in the controversy about "black power" is rooted in a gross imbalance of power and conscience between Negroes and white Americans. It is this distortion, mainly, which is responsible for the widespread, though often inarticulate, assumption that white people are justified in getting what they want through the use of power, but that Negro Americans must, either by nature or by circumstances, make their appeal only through conscience. As a result, the power of white men and the conscience of black men have both been corrupted. The power of white men is corrupted because it meets little meaningful resistance from Negroes to temper it and keep white men from aping God. The conscience of black men is corrupted because, having no power to implement the demands of conscience, the concern for justice is transmuted into a distorted form of love, which, in the absence of justice, becomes chaotic self-surrender. Powerlessness breeds a race of beggars. We are faced now with a situation where conscienceless power meets powerless conscience, threatening the very foundations of our nation.

Therefore, we are impelled by conscience to address at least four groups of people in areas where clarification of the controversy is of the most urgent necessity. We do not claim to present the final word.

It is our hope, however, to communicate meanings from our experience regarding power and certain elements of conscience to help interpret more adequately the dilemma in which we are all involved.

I. To the Leaders of America: Power and Freedom

It is of critical importance that the leaders of this nation listen also to a voice which says that the principal source of the threat to our nation comes neither from the riots erupting in our big cities, nor from the disagreements among the leaders of the civil rights movement, nor even from mere raising of the cry for "black power." These events, we believe, are but the expression of the judgment of God upon our nation for its failure to use its abundant resources to serve the real well-being of people, at home and abroad.

We give our full support to all civil rights leaders as they seek for basically American goals, for we are not convinced that their mutual reinforcement of one another in the past is bound to end in the future. We would hope that the public power of our nation will be used to strengthen the civil rights movement and not to manipulate or further fracture it.

We deplore the overt violence of riots, but we believe it is more important to focus on the real sources of these eruptions. These sources may be abetted inside the ghetto, but their basic causes lie in the silent and covert violence which white middle-class America inflicts upon the victims of the inner city. The hidden, smooth and often smiling decisions of American leaders which tie a white noose of suburbia around the necks, and which pin the backs of the masses of Negroes against the steaming ghetto walls—without jobs in a booming economy; with dilapidated and segregated educational systems in the full view of unenforced laws against it; in short: the failure of American leaders to use American power to create equal opportunity *in life* as well as *in law*—this is the real problem and not the anguished cry for "black power."

From the point of view of the Christian faith, there is nothing necessarily wrong with concern for power. At the heart of the Protestant reformation is the belief that ultimate power belongs to God alone and that men become most inhuman when concentrations of power lead to the conviction—overt or covert—that any nation, race or organization can rival God in this regard. At issue in the relations between whites and Negroes in America is the problem of inequality of power. Out of this imbalance grows the disrespect of white men for the Negro personality and community, and the disrespect of Negroes for themselves. This is a fundamental root of human injustice in America. In one sense, the concept of "black power" reminds us of the need for and the possibility of authentic democracy in America.

We do *not* agree with those who say that we must cease expressing concern for the acquisition of power lest we endanger the "gains" already made by the civil rights movement. The fact of the matter is, there have been few substantive gains since about 1950 in this area. The gap has constantly widened between the incomes of non-whites relative to the whites. Since the Supreme Court decision of 1954, de facto segregation in every major city in our land has increased rather than decreased. Since the middle of the 1950s unemployment among Negroes has gone up rather than down while unemployment has decreased in the white community.

While there has been some progress in some areas for equality for Negroes, this progress has been limited mainly to middle-class Negroes who represent only a small minority of the larger Negro community.

These are the hard facts that we must all face together. Therefore, we must not take the position that we can continue in the same old paths.

When American leaders decide to serve the real welfare of people instead of war and destruction; when American leaders are forced to make the rebuilding of our cities first priority on the nation's agenda; when American leaders are forced by the American people to quit misusing and abusing American power; then will the cry for "black power" become inaudible, for the framework in which all power in America operates would include the power and experience of black men as well as those of white men. In that way, the fear of the power of each group would be removed. America is our beloved homeland. But, America is not God. Only God can do everything. America and the other nations of the world must decide which among a number of alternatives they will choose.

II. To White Churchmen: Power and Love

As black men who were long ago forced out of the white church to create and to wield "black power," we fail to understand the emotional quality of the outcry of some clergy against the use of the term today. It is not enough to answer that "integration" is the solution. For it is precisely the nature of the operation of power under some forms of integration which is being challenged. The Negro Church was created as a result of the refusal to submit to the indignities of a false kind of "integration" in which all power was in the hands of white people. A more equal sharing of power is precisely what is required as the precondition of authentic human interaction. We understand the growing demand of Negro and white youth for a more honest kind of integration; one which increases rather than decreases the capacity of the disinherited to participate with power in all of the structures of our common life. Without this capacity to *participate with power*—i.e., to have some organized political and economic strength to really influence people with whom one interacts—integration is not meaningful. For the issue is not one of racial balance but of honest interracial interaction.

For this kind of interaction to take place, all people need power, whether black or white. We regard as sheer hypocrisy or as a blind and dangerous illusion the view that opposes love to power. Love should be a controlling element in power, but what love opposes is precisely the misuse and abuse of power, not power itself. So long as white churchmen continue to moralize and misinterpret Christian love, so long will justice continue to be subverted in this land.

III. To Negro Citizens: Power and Justice

Both the anguished cry for "black power" and the confused emotional response to it can be understood if the whole controversy is put in the context of American history. Especially must we understand the irony involved in the pride of Americans regarding their ability to act as individuals on the one hand, and their tendency to act as members of ethnic groups on the other hand. In the tensions of this part of our history is revealed both the tragedy and the hope of human redemption in America.

America has asked its Negro citizens to fight for opportunity *as individuals* whereas at certain points in our history what we have needed most has been opportunity for the whole group, not just for selected and approved Negroes. Thus in 1863, the slaves were made legally free, as individuals, but the real question regarding personal and group power to maintain that freedom was pushed aside. Power at that time for a mainly rural people meant land and tools to work the land. In the words of Thaddeus Stevens, power meant "40 acres and a mule". But this power was not made available to the slaves and we see the results today in the pushing of a landless peasantry off the farms into big cities where they come in search mainly of the power to be free. What they find are only the formalities of unenforced legal freedom. So we must ask, "what is the nature of the power which we seek and need today?" Power today is essentially organizational power. It is not a thing lying about in the streets to be fought over. It is a thing which, in some measure, already belongs to Negroes and which must be developed by Negroes in relationship with the great resources of this nation.

Getting power necessarily involves reconciliation. We must first be reconciled to ourselves lest we fail to recognize the resources we already have and upon which we can build. We must be reconciled to ourselves as persons and to ourselves as an historical group. This means we must find our way to a new self-image in which we can feel a normal sense of pride in self, including our variety of skin color and the manifold textures of our hair. As long as we are filled with hatred for ourselves we will be unable to respect others.

At the same time, if we are seriously concerned about power then we must build upon that which we already have. "Black power" is already present to some extent in the Negro church, in Negro fraternities and sororities, in our professional associations, and in the opportunities afforded to Negroes who make decisions in some of the integrated organizations of our society.

We understand the reasons by which these limited forms of "black power" have been rejected by some of our people. Too often the Negro church has stirred its members away from the reign of God in *this world* to a distorted and complacent view of *an otherworldly* conception of God's power. We commit ourselves as churchmen to make more meaningful in the life of our institution our conviction that Jesus Christ reigns in the "here" and "now" as well as in the future he brings in upon us. We shall, therefore, use more of the resources of our churches in working for human justice in the places of social change and upheaval where our Master is already at work.

At the same time, we would urge that Negro social and professional organizations develop new roles for engaging the problem of equal opportunity and put less time into the frivolity of idle chatter and social waste.

We must not apologize for the existence of this form of group power, for we have been oppressed as a group, not as individuals. We will not find our way out of that oppression until both we and America accept the need for Negro Americans as well as for Jews, Italians, Poles and white Anglo-Saxon Protestants, among others, to have and to wield group power.

However, if power is sought merely as an end in itself, it tends to turn upon those who seek it. Negroes need power in order to participate more effectively at all levels of the life of our nation. We are glad that none of those civil rights leaders who have asked for "black power" have suggested that it means a new form of isolationism or a foolish effort at domination. But we must be clear about why we need to be reconciled with the white majority. It is *not* because we are only one-tenth of the population in America; for we do not need to be reminded of the awesome power wielded by the 90% majority. We see and feel that power every day in the destructions heaped upon our families and upon the nation's cities. We do not need to be threatened by such cold and heartless statements. For we are men, not children, and we are growing out of our fear of that power, which can hardly hurt us any more in the future than it does in the present or has in the past. Moreover, those bare figures conceal the potential political strength which is ours if we organize properly in the big cities and establish effective alliances.

Neither must we rest our concern for reconciliation with our white brothers on the fear that failure to do so would damage gains already made by the civil rights movement. If those gains are in fact real, they will withstand the claims of our people for power and justice, not just for a few select Negroes here and there, but for the masses of our citizens. We must rather rest our concern for reconciliation on the firm ground that we and all other Americans *are* one. Our history and destiny are indissolubly linked. If the future is to belong to any of us, it must be prepared for all of us whatever our racial or religious background. For in the final analysis, we are *persons* and the power of all groups must be wielded to make visible our common humanity.

The future of America will belong to neither white nor black unless all Americans work together at the task of rebuilding our cities. We must organize not only among ourselves but with other groups in order that we can, together, gain power sufficient to change this nation's sense of what is *now* important and what must be done *now*. We must work with the remainder of the nation to organize whole cities for the task of making the rebuilding of our cities first priority in the use of our resources. This is more important than who gets to the moon first or the war in Vietnam.

To accomplish this task we cannot expend our energies in spastic or ill-tempered explosions without meaningful goals. We must move from the politics of philanthropy to the politics of metropolitan development for equal opportunity. We must relate all groups of the city together in new ways in order that the truth of our cities might be laid bare and in order that, together, we can lay claim to the great resources of our nation to make truth more human.

IV. To the Mass Media: Power and Truth

The ability or inability of all people in America to understand the upheavals of our day depends greatly on the way power and truth operate in the mass media. During the Southern demonstrations for civil rights, you men of the communications industry performed an invaluable service for the entire country by revealing plainly to our ears and eyes, the ugly truth of a brutalizing system of overt discrimination and segregation. Many of you were mauled and injured, and it took courage for you to stick with the task. You were instruments of change and not merely purveyors of unrelated facts. You were able to do this by dint of personal courage and by reason of the power of national news agencies which supported you.

Today, however, your task and ours is more difficult. The truth that needs revealing today is not so clear-cut in its outlines, nor is there a national consensus to help you form relevant points of view. Therefore, nothing is now more important than that you look for a variety of sources of truth in order that the limited perspectives of all of us might be corrected. Just as you related to a broad spectrum of people in Mississippi instead of relying only on police records and establishment figures, so must you operate in New York City, Chicago and Cleveland.

The power to support you in this endeavor *is present* in our country. It must be searched out. We desire to use our limited influence to help relate you to the variety of experience in the Negro community so that limited controversies are not blown up into the final truth about us. The fate of this country is, to no small extent, dependent upon how you interpret the crises upon us, so that human truth is disclosed and human needs are met.

SIGNATORIES:

Bishop John D. Bright, Sr., AME Church, First Episcopal District, Philadelphia, Pennsylvania

The Rev. John Bryan, Connecticut Council of Churches, Hartford, Connecticut

Suffragan Bishop John M. Burgess, The Episcopal Church, Boston, Massachusetts

The Rev. W. Sterling Cary, Grace Congregational Church, New York, N.Y.

The Rev. Charles E. Cobb, St. John Church (UCC), Springfield, Mass.

The Rev. Caesar D. Coleman, Christian Methodist Episcopal Church, Memphis, Tennessee

The Rev. Joseph C. Coles, Williams Institutional C.M.E. Church, New York, New York

The Rev. George A. Crawley, Jr., St. Paul Baptist Church, Baltimore, Maryland

The Rev. O. Herbert Edwards, Trinity Baptist Church, Baltimore, Md.

The Rev. Bryant George, United Presbyterian Church in the U.S.A., New York, New York

Bishop Charles F. Golden, The Methodist Church, Nashville, Tenn.

The Rev. Quinland R. Gordon, The Episcopal Church, New York, N.Y.

The Rev. James Hargett, Church of Christian Fellowship, U.C.C., Los Angeles, Calif.

The Rev. Edler Hawkins, St. Augustine Presbyterian Church, New York, New York

The Rev. Reginald Hawkins, United Presbyterian Church, Charlotte, North Carolina

Dr. Anna Arnold Hedgeman, Commission on Religion and Race, National Council of Churches, New York, New York

The Rev. R. E. Hood, Gary, Indiana

The Rev. H. R. Hughes, Bethel A.M.E. Church, New York, N.Y.

The Rev. Kenneth Hughes, St. Bartholomew's Episcopal Church, Cambridge, Massachusetts

The Rev. Donald G. Jacobs, St. James A.M.E. Church, Cleveland, Ohio

The Rev. J. L. Joiner, Emanuel A.M.E. Church, New York, New York

The Rev. Arthur A. Jones, Metropolitan A.M.E. Church, Philadelphia, Pennsylvania

The Rev. Stanley King, Sabathini Baptist Church, Minneapolis, Minn.

The Rev. Earl Wesley Lawson, Emanual Baptist Church, Malden, Mass.

The Rev. David Licorish, Abyssinian Baptist Church, New York, N.Y.

The Rev. Arthur B. Mack, St. Thomas A.M.E.Z. Church, Haverstraw, N.Y.

The Rev. James W. Mack, South United Church of Christ, Chicago, Ill.

The Rev. O. Clay Maxwell, Jr., Baptist Ministers Conference of New York City and Vicinity, New York, New York

The Rev. Leon Modeste, the Episcopal Church, New York, N.Y.

Bishop Noah W. Moore, Jr., The Methodist Church, Southwestern Area, Houston, Texas

The Rev. David Nickerson, Episcopal Society for Cultural and Racial Unity, Atlanta, Georgia

The Rev. LeRoy Patrick, Bethesda United Presbyterian Church, Pittsburgh, Pennsylvania

The Rev. Benjamin F. Payton, Commisson on Religion and Race, National Council of Churches, New York, New York

The Rev. Isaiah P. Pogue, St. Mark's Presbyterian Church, Cleveland, Ohio

The Rev. Sandy F. Ray, Empire Baptist State Convention, Brooklyn, N.Y.

Bishop Herbert B. Shaw, Presiding Bishop, Third Episcopal District, A.M.E.Z. Church, Wilmington, N.C.

The Rev. Stephen P. Spottswood, Commission on Race and Cultural Relations, Detroit Council of Churches, Detroit, Michigan

The Rev. Henri A. Stines, Church of the Atonement, Washington, D.C.

Bishop James S. Thomas, Resident Bishop, Iowa Area, The Methodist Church, Des Moines, Iowa

The Rev. V. Simpson Turner, Mt. Carmel Baptist Church, Brooklyn, N.Y.

The Rev. Edgar Ward, Grace Presbyterian Church, Chicago, Ill.

The Rev. Paul M. Washington, Church of the Advocate, Philadelphia, Pa.

The Rev. Frank L. Williams, Methodist Church, Baltimore, Maryland

The Rev. John W. Williams, St. Stephen's Baptist Church, Kansas City, Mo.

The Rev. Gayraud Wilmore, United Presbyterian Church U.S.A., New York, N.Y.

The Rev. M. L. Wilson, Covenant Baptist Church, New York, New York

The Rev. Robert H. Wilson, Corresponding Secretary, National Baptist Convention of America, Dallas, Texas

The Rev. Nathan Wright, Episcopal Diocese of Newark, Newark, N.J.

(Organizational affiliation given for identification purposes only.)

NOTES

Chapter 1

1. The tables in this chapter were prepared by William Sayre. The interpretation of the last table is taken from his correspondence; quotation marks are omitted at his request.

2. See "Racial Tinderbox: A Federal Study Finds Unrest Among Negroes Rising in Many Cities," by Monroe W. Karmin, *Wall Street Journal,* January 5, 1966.

3. See *Negro Population: 1965 Estimates and 1970 Projections,* Center for Research in Marketing, Inc.

Chapter 5

1. Dr. Alvin F. Poussaint, Senior Clinician, Tufts University Medical College Psychiatry Clinic, and Southern Field Director of the National Medical Committee for Human Rights, in "Operation Understanding," *Our Sunday Visitor,* October 23, 1966, p. 1.

Chapter 8

1. "Jobs for Negroes," *Business Week,* June 12, 1965, p. 97. Copyright by *Business Week.*

2. Projections assume a national unemployment rate of 3 percent in 1975. The choice of 3 percent unemployment as a basis for these projections does not indicate an endorsement or even a willingness to accept that level of unemployment. Source: U. S. Department of Labor, Bureau of Labor Statistics, *America's Industrial and Occupational Manpower Requirements, 1964–75.*

3. *Technology and the American Economy,* National Commission on Technology, Automation and Economic Progress, 1966, p. 31.

Chapter 9

1. St. Augustine, *City of God,* Book XV, Chapter 16.

2. This is a juxtaposition of two texts.

3. For a more complete discussion of the concept set forth here see *One Bread, One Body* by Nathan Wright, Jr. (New York: Seabury Press, 1962).

4. See *The Trumpet Sounds* by Dr. Anna Arnold Hedgeman (New York: Holt, Rinehart & Winston, 1964).

5. Adam Clayton Powell, Sr., *Upon This Rock* (New York: Abyssinian Church, 1929), p. 107.

INDEX

Index